MARCIA DECOSTER PRESENTS

Interviews with 30 Beaders on Inspiration and Technique

LARK JEWELRY & BEADING

Editor
Nathalie Mornu

Production Editor
Kevin Kopp

Art Director
and Cover Designer
Carol Morse Barnao

Art Intern
Lisa Maddox

**Front cover,
clockwise from top left**

Petra Tismer, Just for Fun, 2011

Siân Nolan, Matryoshka
Needlecase and Annushka
Scissor Charm, 2011

Beki Haley, Enchanted, 2009

Melissa Ingram, Untitled
Appliqué Headband, 2012

Petra Tismer, Golden Sun, 2010

Miriam Shimon,
Indian Sunrise, 2012

Spine

Elke Leonhardt-Rath,
Untitled Pendant, 2012

**Back cover,
clockwise from top left**

Martina Nagele,
Drag! Me! Out!, 2012

Heather Kingsley-Heath,
Little Owl Charms, 2012

Marsha Wiest-Hines,
Missing, 2012

Ann Braginsky, Summer
Garden Hairpin, 2012

Contents Page (opposite)

Heather Kingsley-Heath,
Beaded Beetle and Beaded
Butterfly, 2010
Flowers and Leaves, 2009

**Page 4,
clockwise from top left**

Siân Nolan, Spike Cuff, 2012

Kinga Nichols, Presence #1
and Presence #2, 2012

Petra Tismer, Traveling to
Milwaukee, 2010

Patrizia Tager, Arearea
"Joyousness," 2010

Susan Blessinger, Impending
Bloom, 2011

Page 5

Heather Kingsley-Heath, Little
Owl Charms, 2012

An Imprint of Sterling Publishing
387 Park Avenue South
New York, NY 10016

Text © 2014 by Lark Crafts, an Imprint of Sterling Publishing Co., Inc.

ISBN 978-1-4547-0797-4

Library of Congress Cataloging-in-Publication Data

DeCoster, Marcia.
  Marcia DeCoster presents Interviews with 30 Beaders on Inspiration & Technique.
    pages cm. -- (Spotlight on beading)
  Includes index.
  ISBN 978-1-4547-0797-4
  1. Beadwork. 2. Jewelry making. I. Title. II. Title: Beaded jewelry by
30 international artists.
  TT860.D4235 2014
  745.594'2--dc23

                    2013020011

Distributed in Canada by Sterling Publishing
c/o Canadian Manda Group, 165 Dufferin Street
Toronto, Ontario, Canada M6K 3H6
Distributed in the United Kingdom by GMC Distribution Services
Castle Place, 166 High Street, Lewes, East Sussex, England BN7 1XU
Distributed in Australia by Capricorn Link (Australia) Pty. Ltd.
P.O. Box 704, Windsor, NSW 2756, Australia

For information about custom editions, special sales, and premium and corporate purchases, please contact Sterling Special Sales at 800-805-5489 or specialsales@sterlingpublishing.com.

Email academic@larkbooks.com for information about desk and examination copies. The complete policy can be found at larkcrafts.com.

Every effort has been made to ensure that all the information in this book is accurate. However, due to differing conditions, tools, and individual skills, the publisher cannot be responsible for any injuries, losses, and other damages that may result from the use of the information in this book.

Manufactured in China

2 4 6 8 10 9 7 5 3 1

larkcrafts.com

contents

introduction

this book has grown out of my continuing amazement over the remarkable associations and connections being formed among the worldwide beading community. With the advent of the digital age, including the proliferation of communication channels such as web pages, blogs, and social media sites, I have been able to develop wonderful ongoing relationships with beaders across the United States, South Africa, Germany, Israel, Canada, Singapore, Australia, and more. We have connected over our love of beads, so I thought it would be really fun and informative to ask many of my fellow beaders about their methods, processes, and inspirations . . . and also how *they* use the Internet.

The interviews that follow, along with brief biographies and photos that showcase each artist's work, are the results of this effort. You will also find responses to a number of questions about these beaders' design careers, their passions, what artistic directions they'd like to explore, and their favorite materials and techniques, as well as the answer to a question that is unique to the work each does with beads.

The wonder of the Internet has given me the means not only to admire beadwork from around the world, but to share illustration tips, compare bead sources, mourn losses as well as celebrate successes with beading colleagues, and marvel at the interconnectedness of it all when mutual friends are discovered. It is with great delight that I've had the opportunity to meet in person many of the friends I've made online, and then been able to maintain these connections and let my relationships continue to flourish.

I keep in contact with this collection of artists, and many others, on a regular basis as members of our incredibly supportive online beading community—a community not unlike one you might find in a local bead society or a national show, where like-minded people connect over their love for beads. Each morning I reach out globally to online friends and am grateful for the words and photos and love that we exchange.

So in these pages you will find different styles of beadwork, from Nancy Dale's elaborate fringe to Heather Collin's cubic right angle weave creations and Susan Blessinger's multimedia masterpieces; from Gabriella van Diepen's eclectic use of materials to Miriam Shimon's bold use of color and Martina Nagele's humor-infused beadwork: thirty different artists in all!

I admire the beadwork of each person featured in these pages, and I've chosen some of their most exciting pieces to share. It is my hope that you enjoy the beauty, richness, and diversity of the work that each artist creates, and celebrate the incredibly artistic global community represented here.

I am a U.S. citizen who was born and raised in Thailand. From childhood I was exposed to the beautiful, intricate items that are part of traditional Thai art. Metalwork, enamelware, gem-studded jewelry, and gorgeous woven textiles were part of my everyday experience. I have worked as a bead artist and teacher in the Seattle area since 2000. My work has been recognized a number of times in *Beadwork* magazine and in Marcia DeCoster's book, *Beaded Opulence*. I received the K. Gottfried prize in 2007.

A

daeng weaver

"My beadweaving revolves exclusively around jewelry making. I love being able to produce wearable art."

B

C

A *Alexandra Bangle*, 2012
9 x 2 x 2 cm
Seed beads, vinyl tube, gem-stones, polyethylene thread; right angle weave
Photo by Chareon Suwanngate

B *Eternity*, 2011
9 x 2 x 1.5 cm
Round seed beads, ruby ron-delle, sapphire rondelle, small sapphires; peyote stitch, right angle weave
Photo by Chareon Suwanngate

C *Sedona Sky Pendant*, 2006
8.2 x 4.3 x 1 cm
Cylinder beads, seed beads, turquoise, small pearls, cubic zirconia, polyethylene thread; peyote stitch
Photo by Chareon Suwanngate

YOUR USE OF GEMSTONES IN BEAD-WEAVING IS UNIQUE. WHAT FIRST INSPIRED YOU TO INCORPORATE GEMSTONES?
The use of beautiful gemstones is a part of traditional Thai jewelry. It was natural for me to turn to precious and semiprecious stones for embellishment of seed bead jewelry and to make larger gemstones a focus in my beadwork designs.

GIVE US TWO SENTENCES TO CHARACTERIZE YOUR WORK.
My work combines the humble seed bead with precious gems and met-als to create elegant jewelry. Beads are my sole artistic medium, and I wouldn't want it any other way.

WHAT GIVES YOU INSPI-RATION FOR CREATING YOUR JEWELRY?
Thai art, particularly small portable enamel-ware and jewelry, but also the architecture of Buddhist temples, because of the exquisite colors and gold with which they are embellished.

WHAT'S YOUR METHOD FOR DEVELOPING DESIGNS?
My work is very struc-tural despite the predominance of color. I experiment with many possible designs to en-sure my pieces will be

strong as well as beautiful. I am meticulous about building patterns based upon numerical relationships that I find are critical to pattern symmetry as well as strength. Much preparation is required to make a beautiful design.

WE ARE INTERESTED IN YOUR USE OF THE INTERNET AND SOCIAL MEDIA. WHAT CAN YOU TELL US?
Actually, I have only recently begun to post photos of my work on Facebook. What's interesting is that I've been contacted by people I don't know who love my beadwork and have been responding favorably to it.

HOW WOULD YOU LIKE YOUR JEWELRY TO AFFECT THOSE WHO SEE IT?
I hope viewers experience some of the delight I experience while I am making my jewelry. I am continually amazed and surprised by the beauty of the many possible combinations of beads and gemstones waiting to be discovered.

ARE THERE OTHER FORMS OF ARTISTIC MEDIA YOU LIKE TO WORK WITH?
I've explored some in needlework, particularly embroidery. My first experience with beads was traditional Chinese pearl knotting.

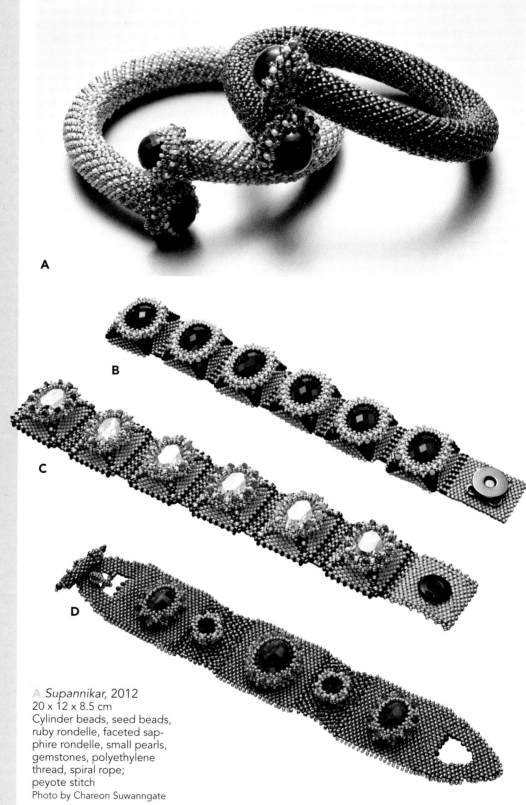

A

B

C

D

A *Supannikar*, 2012
20 x 12 x 8.5 cm
Cylinder beads, seed beads, ruby rondelle, faceted sapphire rondelle, small pearls, gemstones, polyethylene thread, spiral rope; peyote stitch
Photo by Chareon Suwanngate

B *Black Baguette Bracelet*, 2011
19 x 2.5 x 1 cm
Cylinder beads, seed beads, polyethylene thread, crystals, pearls, turquoise, snap; peyote stitch
Photo by Chareon Suwanngate

C *Lumierre*, 2011
19 x 2 x 1.3 cm
Cylinder seed beads, crystals, polyethylene thread, snap, gemstones (ruby, emerald, sapphire), pearls; peyote stitch
Photo by Chareon Suwanngate

D *Aida Bracelet*, 2006
20.5 x 4 x 1.5 cm
Cylinder beads, seed beads, polyethylene thread, facetted rubies, pearls, gemstones; peyote stitch, right angle weave, brick stitch
Photo by Chareon Suwanngate

C

E

F

E *Princess Necklace,* 2009
48 x 7.5 x 0.5 cm
Cylinder beads, seed beads,
oval and rondelle gemstones,
pearls; Ndebele stitch,
peyote stitch
Photo by Chareon Suwanngate

F *The Empress Cuff,* 2006
21.5 x 3 x 0.5 cm
Triangle beads, gemstones,
polyethylene thread; herringbone stitch
Photo by Chareon Suwanngate

WHAT MATERIALS DO YOU FIND YOURSELF USING MOST OFTEN?

I am most drawn to pre-
cious and semiprecious
gemstones, cylinder
beads, and seed pearls
of all kinds. I prefer to
use size 11° and size
15° seed beads.

HOW DO YOU CHOOSE BEADS FOR YOUR PIECES?

I usually select ma-
terials that create
a harmonious color
palette with as much
uniformity as pos-
sible because I create
very precise structural
designs. Gemstones
are more natural in
their variations, so it is
important to use great
care in marrying their
irregularities with the
uniformity of machine-
produced glass beads.

"Daeng's use of beau-
tiful gemstones, many
gathered in her native
Thailand, sets her
work apart. Combin-
ing these stones with
warm bronze seed
beads gives the rich
look of fine jewelry."

—MARCIA DECOSTER

I'm a mostly a self-taught bead artist and teacher originally from Denmark who currently lives and works in Israel. My background is in professional makeup, and I enjoy exploring colors and shapes using intricate and detailed designs. My work has been published in numerous magazines. I am best known for my floral beadwork, elaborate soutache work, and use of color. I was a Bead Dreams finalist in 2010 and 2012, and I recently won second place in the British Bead Awards.

miriamshimon.etsy.com

A

miriam shimon

B

A *Alexandrina*, 2012
49 x 12 x 3 cm
Seed beads, cabochons, gold leaves, crystals; soutache embroidery, herringbone stitch
Photo by artist

B *Stella Luminosa*, 2012
50 x 12 x 4 cm
Soutache, seed beads, cabochons; soutache embroidery, herringbone stitch
Photo by artist

C *Aurora*, 2012
50 x 12 x 4 cm
Soutache, seed beads, cabochons, crystals, rhinestone chain; soutache embroidery, herringbone stitch
Photo by artist

c

"I'm always curious to discover new techniques. Nothing is more exciting than starting out with nothing and ending up with something."

I don't have one specific favorite. Rather, I like fusing different techniques so that my work often consists of many different stitches, such as peyote stitch and herringbone stitch. More recently, I have enjoyed bead embroidery and also working with soutache, which has proven to be a versatile medium for expressing my personal artistic point of view.

HOW DID YOU START YOUR BEADING "CAREER?"

I first discovered beadwork five years ago quite by accident. At the time I was experimenting with oil and acrylic paint on canvas and wooden boxes. One day I walked into a craft store to buy supplies and came upon a display of beaded jewelry. My curiosity was piqued. It only took one lesson for me to realize that I had finally found a medium that would challenge my creativity and provide a meditative outlet for my artistic expression. This was a medium where I could finally express myself and never run out of ideas.

WHICH MATERIALS ARE INDISPENSIBLE AS FAR AS YOU ARE CONCERNED?

Hands down, seed beads are the most versatile of the materials I use. I also love crystals in all their shapes and forms; there is something endlessly intriguing and fascinating about the glimmer and luster they provide. My recent work has been focused on the use of soutache threads, along with textiles.

WHERE DOES THE INTERNET FIT INTO YOUR BEADING ARTISTRY?

Living in a small community, I have not had the privilege of meeting many others with a passion for beading, so it has been imperative to learn from the huge fellowship of beaders around the world. Without the Internet, I would never have been exposed to the animated discussions and visual sharing I've received from such a variety of wonderful people. Their kindness, generosity, and friendship play a huge role in my development as an artist. I have learned more from my fellow beaders than from any single book or magazine. Watching in awe at what can be achieved by putting thread and needle to a pile of shiny

A

B

A *Indian Sunrise*, 2012
48 x 7 x 5 cm
Soutache, seed beads, crystals, flat cabochons; soutache embroidery, herringbone stitch
Photo by artist

B *Misty Autumn Bracelet*, 2012
19 x 6 cm
Soutache, seed beads, crystals, cabochons; soutache embroidery
Photo by artist

C

D

C *Tangerine Summer Bloom*, 2012
50 x 7 x 4 cm
Seed beads, crystal drops, crystals; net weave, peyote stitch
Photo by artist

D *Misty Autumn Necklace*, 2012
50 x 8 x 4 cm
Seed beads, crystals, cabochons, crystal drops; right angle weave, soutache embroidery
Photo by artist

small beads has inspired me to take my own path and never be afraid of trying something new.

WHAT IS YOUR MUSE? WHERE DOES CREATIVITY SPRING FROM?
Inspiration is everywhere, whether in music, interior design, or even a beautifully plated dish in a restaurant. My primary and most constant source has always been nature and its bounty of floral beauty. I'm fascinated with the shapes and colors of flowers and trees.

Also, I often look for inspiration in music, from the quiet Romantic work of Chopin and the emotional thunder of Rachmaninoff, to contemporary rock and jazz—every musical style conveys its own mood and inspiration. I have many pieces of jewelry in my collection that were directly influenced by the music I was listening to at the time of their creation.

I'M CURIOUS HOW YOU VIEW YOUR OWN WORK.
I would say it is mainly wearable modern romantic. I love French Impressionist painting. Pastel colors and serenity are elements I'm constantly drawn to, whether it is in beadwork or paint. I also like creating art that can be worn comfortably and isn't too overpowering.

It is a welcome challenge to find ways of achieving a perfect balance between imagination and sensibility, between glamorous and approachable.

DO YOU HAVE EXPERIENCE WORKING ARTISTICALLY WITH OTHER MEDIA?

For many years I worked as a professional makeup artist. It was my love of color and painting that initially drew me to it, and that work has definitely translated into my beaded art. Making the transition from a two-dimensional to a multidimensional medium has provided me with a whole new perspective on art in general.

TELL US YOUR THOUGHTS ON THE CREATIVE PROCESS AS IT PERTAINS TO YOUR WORK.

I don't make any drawings in advance and I hardly ever plan a design. For me, the process is quite organic, although somewhat disorganized. I usually start with an idea that revolves around a color scheme. Next, I decide on the materials I want to use, then choose a focal point and advance bit by bit. It can change and develop many times before I'm comfortable with the result, and I spend a lot of time contemplating the harmony of each step in the process.

A

B

A *Chocolate Twirl Necklace*, 2012
48 x 8 x 4 cm
Seed beads, leaves, cabochon; twisted flat herringbone stitch, fringing
Photo by artist

B *Vica Pendant*, 2012
48 x 9 x 7 cm
Soutache, seed beads, cube beads, beaded beads; soutache embroidery
Photo by artist

C *Eye of the Nile*
Pendant, 2012
6 x 5 cm
Cabochons, crystals, seed
beads; soutache embroidery
Photo by artist

D *Michal*, 2012
50 x 7 x 2 cm
Soutache, seed beads,
crystals, cabochons, baroque
drop; right angle weave,
soutache embroidery
Photo by artist

C

D

**HOW DO YOU GO ABOUT
SELECTING THE BEADS
YOU WANT TO USE?**
I always choose beads
based on color. Once
I'm satisfied with the
color combination, I
then select the right
shape and size from my
endless stash. I never
end up using all the
beads I had originally
planned because things
always change. It is
precisely that dynamic
process that is a con-
stant source of beading
joy and fun.

**HOW DO YOU HOPE TO
INSPIRE PEOPLE WHO
SEE YOUR WORK?**
I hope that any of my
pieces brings about the
feelings of peace and
harmony from which
it was created. I want
to produce a sense of
tranquility and inner
reflection, an apprecia-
tion for the ancient art
of beadweaving and its
modern applications.

"All the elements of
Miriam's jewelry seem
to flow seamlessly into
one another, provid-
ing a sense of serene
beauty and wonder."

—MARCIA DECOSTER

patrick duggan

"A beading friend tells me when I struggle with a piece it usually ends up being a very good design."

I have always enjoyed making things with my hands, even as a boy. Consequently, as an adult, I have exhibited and sold paintings, drawings, and sculptures. Then, in 2007, I discovered my passion for jewelry making, particularly beadweaving, in which I have since begun to teach workshops. My designs have won competition awards and my patterns have been published in international magazines. I dream of authoring a best-selling book on beadweaving design.

patrickduggandesigns.com

A

A *La Femme*, 2012
30 x 6 cm
Crystal drop, Czech glass,
seed beads; herringbone stitch,
peyote stitch
Photo by Neva Brown

B *Regalia*, 2012
27 x 17 cm
Crystal rivolis, crystal drops and
bicones, seed beads; herringbone
stitch, peyote stitch
Photo by Neva Brown

C *Sputnik—Beaded Bead*, 2012
4 x 4 x 4 cm
Glass pearl, spikes, crystal bicones,
seed beads; no particular stitch
Photo by Neva Brown

D *Sophia*, 2011
33 x 16 cm
Seed beads, montées, vintage
German Lucite; right angle weave,
peyote stitch
Photo by Neva Brown

DOES DESIGNING WOMEN'S JEWELRY PRESENT ANY SPECIAL CHALLENGES?

I often struggle deciding how long a necklace should be, or where a pendant should sit. I guess not being a woman and not wearing what I create causes the difficulty.

WHAT ONE WORD POPS INTO YOUR MIND WHEN THINKING ABOUT YOUR OWN WORK?

I love making all sorts of items, so I'd say eclectic. I may sit down and create something that is incredibly Art Deco; my next piece might look like something worn in the court of Louis XVI before the French Revolution.

DO YOU CONCENTRATE ON MAKING JEWELRY, OR DO YOU LIKE TO MAKE OTHER FORMS OF BEADWORK?

So far my main focus has been jewelry, although I have this idea that a lot of men really like glitter. They won't buy it, though, because they don't wear it. I would like to create small pieces of beading using crystals and rivolis, then frame them or hang them on a wall. Maybe I can gain the male glitz-and-glitter lovers with items they can look at and appreciate.

WHAT GETS YOUR CREATIVE JUICES FLOWING?

Lots of things inspire my creativity: shapes in architecture, colors in nature, other artists, etc. I have that voice in my head that asks, "What would it look like if you did . . . ?"

WHERE DO YOU FIND IDEAS FOR YOUR CREATIVITY?

Where shall I start?! I love fashion, haut-couture, art, architecture, interior design, flowers. Inspiration comes from everywhere. If I keep my eyes open, I find it staring me in the face.

WHEN DID YOU START WITH BEADS?

I began with macramé-beaded wristbands in 2006, then went on to stringing. I discovered beadweaving in 2007 when I learned how to make a spiral rope. I haven't stopped beadweaving since.

HOW HAVE YOUR ONLINE RELATIONSHIPS INFLUENCED YOU?

I find the Internet beading community very supportive and helpful. It is a cyber-family. People are willing to share knowledge and form close connections. They worry about each other, check on each other, have a laugh with each other, and this is wonderful.

I have developed some strong Internet friendships with a number of amazing beadweavers, and their input motivates me and keeps me passionate. Sometimes beading is isolating, so it is beneficial to have another beading buddy with whom I can share concepts and struggles. I have formed a

A *Venetian Mirrors*, 2012
20 x 7.5 cm
Crystal rivolis, montées, bicones, rhodium-plated seed beads; peyote stitch, herringbone stitch
Photo by Neva Brown

B *Gelato*, 2012
36 x 4 cm
Crystal rivoli, glass drops, druk beads, spike, dyed howlite toggle, seed beads; embellished cubic right angle weave, peyote stitch
Photo by artist

C *Gatsby—Art Deco Tribute*, 2012
31 x 7 cm
Crystal rivolis, diamantes, and drops, bicones, rhodium-plated seed beads; herringbone stitch, peyote stitch, cubic right angle weave
Photo by artist

D *Davinia*, 2012
30 x 11.5 cm
Crystal drop, square, round and bicone crystals, fresh water pearls, shell pearls, seed beads, 24-karat gold-plated seed beads, slide clasp; cubic right angle weave, peyote stitch
Photo by Neva Brown

E *Madame's Favourite*, 2012
55 x 7 cm
Crystal bicones, shell pearls (inside), glass drops, super-duos, seed beads; embellished cubic right angle weave, peyote stitch
Photo by Neva Brown

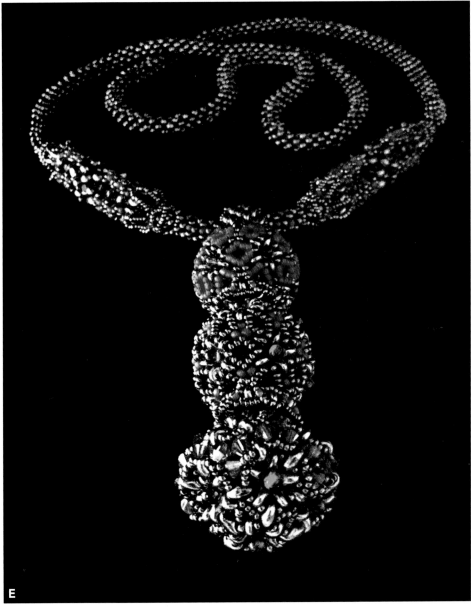

good friendship with fellow Australian Melissa Ingram (see page 24). We share our ideas and creations with each other.

WHAT EMOTIONAL IMPACT DO YOU AIM TO DELIVER TO YOUR AUDIENCE?

I love that sudden intake of breath when they first see a design. I don't just seek the "WOW factor;" I want the "GASP factor." The wow follows the gasp!

WHAT ARE YOUR FAVORITE MATERIALS TO USE?

Seed beads! Love them—can't get enough of them. I prefer seed beads with rounded edges. I also like crystals for lots of sparkle.

WHAT OTHER ARTISTIC ACTIVITIES DO YOU ENJOY?

I was knitting beanies at age ten. I taught myself crochet, tatting, and macramé, so thread work was big when I was younger. As an adult, I have exhibited paintings, drawings, and clay sculpture.

"Patrick uses his huge repertoire of technical skills to create beautifully shaped components that he brings together in his gorgeous and regal jewelry."

—MARCIA DECOSTER

A

I have been a beadwork designer for about 12 years, living in Mansfield, England, and my work has been published in numerous books and magazines around the world. I particularly enjoy the challenges of three-dimensional beadwork; consequently, I began in 2011 to predominantly work with beads of only one color in order to fully explore the possibilities of shaped beadwork. I teach beadwork internationally and sell patterns from my website.

kerrieslade.co.uk

kerrie slade

"I hope that my work comes across as intricate and innovative in design, with elegant, unfussy results that belie the work involved—with a little bit of English eccentricity thrown in for good measure."

B

A *Four Flower Pins,* 2012
3 x 3 x 1 cm each
Cylinder beads, pearls, assorted beads, thread, sterling silver; brick stitch
Photo by artist

B *Peacock Pearl Lariat,* 2011
Lariat: 104 x 0.5 cm;
Flowers: 4 cm
Seed beads, cylinder beads, pearls, thread; brick stitch, peyote stitch
Photo by artist

C *Guardian of the Garden,* 2011
Necklace: 73 cm;
Pendant: 11 x 3 cm
Seed beads, pearls, amazonite carving, thread, silver; herringbone stitch, spiral rope stitch, fringing, surface embellishment
Photo by artist

D *From Midnight Oaks Magic Acorns Grow,* 2012
16 x 2 x 3 cm
Seed beads, gumdrop beads, thread, ribbon; brick stitch, ladder stitch, peyote stitch
Photo by artist

C

D

HOW LONG HAVE BEADS BEEN YOUR MEDIUM FOR CREATING ART?

I have been beading since 2001, but it really started as a hobby. I never considered myself to be an artist, and I am still growing into my artist's skin.

I LIKE HOW YOU EXAMINE STRUCTURE BY WORKING WITH BEADS IN ONE COLOR. WHAT IS THAT LIKE?

I wanted to open my mind to explore new ideas, so I gave myself one year to create a themed body of work in just one color. But I enjoyed it so much that I have carried the idea beyond the year! I used to spend more time choosing color combinations than I would creating the actual piece of beadwork—so I simply took color out of the equation. Rather than limiting me, this has actually given me great freedom. Now I focus on the shape I want to achieve, concentrate on the stitches, and look for materials that complement my palette.

HOW DO YOU USUALLY MAKE YOUR BEAD CHOICES?

Well for the collection illustrated here, color is the main criterion. But generally my decisions are based on the love-at-first-sight factor, followed by quality and availability.

YOU KNOW I'M PARTICULARLY INTERESTED IN THE ROLE THE INTERNET PLAYS IN YOUR ART.

Yes, the Internet plays a huge part. In addition to selling, I admire amazing and inspirational bead-work from around the world. I especially enjoy seeing works in progress to glimpse other people's design processes. Also, I have formed some truly great and lasting friendships, mainly thanks to Facebook. Being able to see people's photos (of their work or their families) and to read their status updates about what makes them happy or sad really helps me know them and connect. I appreciate the way the Internet enables us to share our triumphs and failures as well as our knowledge and support.

HOW DO IDEAS FOR CREATIONS COME TO MIND?

I have always been inspired by nature, especially flowers and leaves. When I started creating my "Midnight Garden" collection, I wanted a theme besides being monochromatic, so I continued with the natural world idea, but added a dash of fantasy. Immersing myself in this whimsical bead world helps me cope with the sometimes harsh realities of life.

HOW DO YOU GET STARTED ON A PROJECT?

Usually an idea pops into my head and I visualize it perfectly completed in beadwork. I think, "Oh, I'll just do a bit of herring-bone and add some brick stitch and sew on some pearls." And often nothing works quite the way I envisioned, so there is a lot of trial and error.

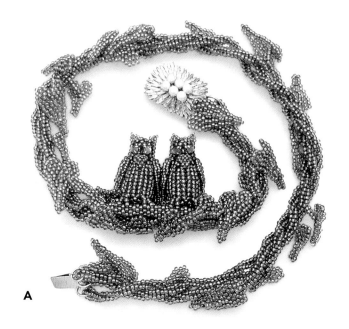

A

B

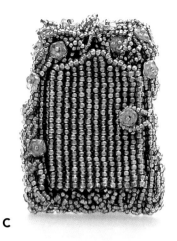

C

D

E

A *The Family Tree,* 2012
52 x 3 cm
Seed beads, crystals, thread, silver; herringbone stitch, brick stitch, ladder stitch
Photo by artist

B *Gateway to the Garden,* 2011
Necklace: 42 x 0.5 cm; Pendant: 5 x 4 x 1 cm
Seed beads, cabochon, pearls, thread,
silver; herringbone stitch, brick stitch,
surface embellishment
Photo by artist

C *Fairy Doorway Pin; Pendant,* 2012
6 x 4 x 1 cm
Seed beads, cabochon, pressed-glass
beads, thread, silver; herringbone stitch,
square stitch, surface embellishment
Photo by artist

D *Mr. and Mrs. Prickles,* 2012
3 x 4 x 6 cm
Seed beads, dagger beads, twin beads,
crystals, thread; herringbone stitch,
surface embellishment
Photo by artist

E *Midnight Daisy Pin,* 2011
8 x 5 x 1 cm
Seed beads, cylinder beads, thread, silver;
brick stitch, peyote stitch, ladder stitch
Photo by artist

**WHAT NEW BEAD TECH-
NIQUES DO YOU LOOK
FORWARD TO TRYING?**
I usually turn to my
old favorites of brick
stitch and herringbone
with a bit of peyote
and ladder stitch, but I
want to try some other
stitches, particularly
cubic right angle weave,
because that seems to
have great potential for
sculptural beadwork.

**WHAT ARE YOUR FAVOR-
ITE MATERIALS?**
My top would be seed
or cylinder beads, usu-
ally in sizes 11° or 15°,
because I like to create
the base of each piece
purely from beads. I
am also very fond of
pearls (especially tiny
seed pearls in a peacock
finish), crystals, and
unusual clasps. I am
always on the lookout
for special items, such
as the amazonite carved
owl that I included in
my "Guardian of the
Garden" piece (page 21).

"There is an unfussy
simplicity and a sweetly
romantic quality to the
body of work that
Kerrie has created."

—MARCIA DECOSTER

A

melissa ingram

I am a full-time beadwork artist, project designer, instructor, and a zealous collector of vintage Swarovski elements and antique beads. My projects and articles have appeared regularly in *Australian Beading Magazine* since 2008. I joined the design team with Australia's first all-digital magazine, *Digital Beading Magazine*, in 2012.

I have won national and international awards, and my work has appeared in several Lark books, including *Showcase 500 Beaded Jewelry, 500 Art Necklaces,* and *Soutache,* as well as in other titles yet to be released.

aussiebeader.com

B

A *Melbournian,* 2011
37 x 8.5 x 2.5 cm
Seed beads, drop beads, glass drops, glass pearls, stones, cosmic rings, navette pendants, rondelles, column pendants, bicones, pearls, polyethylene thread, tube armature, magnetic clasp; peyote stitch, herringbone stitch, picot stitch
Photo by artist

B Untitled appliqué headband, 2012
Appliqué, 12.5 x 9 x 3 cm
Seed beads, antique bugle beads, glass drops, peridot gemstone, coin beads, machined appliqué, metal meshed wire headband, beading foundation, synthetic suede; embroidery stitches, single bead edging stitch
Photo by artist

C *Tequila Sunrise,* 2012
42.5 x 24.5 x 3.5 cm
Seed beads, crystal pendant beads, drop beads, bicones, vintage montées and stones, pearls, top-drilled bicones, vintage chatons, cosmic ring, rondelles, polyethylene thread, tube armature, gold-filled cones; cubic right angle weave, right angle weave, herringbone stitch, peyote stitch, picot stitch
Photo by artist

C

"I rotate a design in my mind as if I were running a CAD software program. I visualize thread paths and often anticipate design problems before I actually thread a bead."

I FIND YOUR WORK TO HAVE A WONDERFUL FEMININE QUALITY. WOULD YOU AGREE?

Feminine, yes, I can see that. Even more, my beadwork is carefully created with love and devotion to make what I feel are unique and bold designs. My designs often incorporate structural and engineered components and elements and can be described as dramatic—the ideas behind opera diva and red carpet come to mind.

TELL US ABOUT YOUR EXPERIENCE AS A BEAD ARTIST.

I discovered beads more than 20 years ago, but used them merely for strung designs and beaded appliqués for clothing. In 2004 I fell in love with off-loom beadweaving, but it was not until 2007 that I taught myself peyote stitch. Gradually, I have mastered more and more stitches.

HAVE YOU WORKED WITH OTHER MEDIA TO CREATE JEWELRY?

I deeply enjoy the process of working with two-part epoxy resin and use it purely as a means of sealing images within the resin, thus forming my own cabochons. Soutache embroidery is my other love, and I have explored using polymer clay and precious metal clay within my beadwork.

HOW DO YOU DISCOVER IDEAS FOR NEW DESIGNS?

Sometimes I cannot identify where inspiration comes from, but I do enjoy vintage couture costume jewelry from the great designers. Art Nouveau, Art Deco, and Arabesque styles stimulate my thinking. I seek color inspiration from Mother Nature.

DO CERTAIN BEADS APPEAL TO YOU MORE THAN OTHERS?

Premium Japanese and Czech seed beads, and anything Swarovski. Also, vintage and antique beads hold such mystery that I am drawn to them because of the history they invoke—I have a huge collection of vintage and discontinued Swarovski elements. I do not use any bead that is not colorfast or galvanized.

WHAT IS YOUR METHOD FOR WORKING OUT A DESIGN IDEA?

Sometimes I will sketch ideas for different design options, which can lead to additional ideas. Then the beads take over as I begin working with them and they make their limitations or opportunities known through the creative journey. My designs may morph from one phase to the next and end up with only a few features that resemble the initial design.

A

A *Midas Tidepools,* 2010
49 x 13 x 2.5 cm
Cylinder beads, seed beads, bicones, pearls, round stones, rondelles, lampworked beads, various glass beads, vintage glass micro pearl beads, vintage mother-of-pearl button, polyethylene thread; peyote stitch, right angle weave, tubular herringbone stitch, netting
Photo by TWK Studios

B *Arabesque Armour,* 2012
50 x 21 x 3.5 cm
Seed beads, vintage chatons, rivolis, bicones, pearls, round beads, chessboard beads, briolettes, long oval stones, recycled gold-plated beads, pendants, enameled metal chain, glass drops, polyethylene thread, tube and wire armature, gold-filled magnetic clasps; cubic right angle weave, peyote stitch
Photo by TWK Studios

B

DOES THE INTERNET AFFECT YOUR BEAD ART?
Yes, the Internet is very exciting. I connect with like-minded devotees over the world—gotta love that! Facebook in particular has been pivotal in developing my global network of beading artists. I follow blogs, connect with photo streams on sites such as Flickr, and visit the various stores on Etsy.

WHAT CAN YOU TELL US ABOUT THE IMPORTANCE OF ONLINE RELATIONSHIPS?
Meeting Miriam Shimon (see page 10) online influenced my desire to do more than merely research soutache embroidery—I began to start making soutache samples. The Soutache Embroidery workshops I taught at the Aussie Beading Retreat 2012 were titled "Miriam" in her honor. I also share a unique friendship with fellow Australian designer Patrick Duggan (see page 16). We communicate almost daily and share new designs at various stages of construction.

A *Lashed Lily*, 2011
35 x 5.5 x 3.5 cm
Seed beads, drop beads, bicones,
cosmic square, lily pendants, pearls,
magnetic clasp, tube armature, polyethylene thread; right angle weave,
herringbone stitch, peyote stitch, picot
stitch
Photo by TWK Studios

B *Hero*, 2012
28 x 9.5 x 2.5 cm
Seed beads, drop beads, cosmic
squares, pearls, bicones, rondelles,
magnetic clasp, polyethylene thread,
wire; right angle weave, cubic right
angle weave, tubular right angle weave,
peyote stitch, herringbone stitch
Photo by artist

C

D

C *Lil' Birdie Soutache
Pendant*, 2012
6 x 3.5 cm
Porcelain cabochon, silk
hand-dyed strap, vintage glass
pearl bead, pearls, soutache,
seed beads, polyethylene
thread, synthetic suede;
free-form beading, single
bead edging stitch
Photo by TWK Studios

D *Tubastreau*, 2010
28.5 x 16.5 x 1 cm
Pearls, round stone, flat
briolettes, aquiline beads,
twist beads, cosmic beads,
rounds, bicones, polyethylene
thread, ribbon; right
angle weave
Photo by TWK Studios

**ARE YOU
EXPERIMENTING WITH
ANY NEW TECHNIQUES?**
Currently, cubic
right angle weave
consumes my focus. I
see infinite potential
for this wonderful
stitch because it allows
me the challenge of
dimensional construction
and engineering. I also
anticipate working more
with soutache.

**HOW DO YOU CHOOSE
WHICH BEADS TO
COLLECT FOR YOUR
STASH?**
My bead stash is
wonderful. I am drawn
to certain beads when
they appeal to me
visually. Even though
I often make bead
purchases via the
Internet, I will take
a current piece of
beadwork to my local
bead store and match
colors and bead styles to
add to the design.

"Melissa's creations
are filled with soft,
complementary color
palettes and intricate
detail to form the
lovely shapes that
grace her beadwork."

—MARCIA DECOSTER

I have been in love with beads for more than 40 years after being introduced to the amazing art form of seed beadweaving by my grandmother. That early start in exploring the intricacy and fine detail that can be attained with seed beads has stayed with me throughout my life. I always teach students about the importance of attention to detail and craftsmanship while helping them explore their natural creativity. The joy that beads bring to my life cannot fully be expressed in words.

BekiHaley.com

A

beki haley

"While I play with other media from time to time, the allure of the beads never allows me to stray very far away."

B

C

D

A *Enchanted*, 2009
6.4 x 1.7 cm
Glass button, crystals, cylinder
beads, seed beads, drop
beads; peyote stitch, netting,
fringing, herringbone stitch
Photo by Shawn Haley

B *Moonflower*, 2012
56 x 11.4 x 1.5 cm
Cylinder beads, seed beads,
chatons; peyote stitch,
St. Petersburg stitch
Photo by Shawn Haley

C *Ancient Seas*, 2008
56 x 15 x 1.2 cm
Ammonites, seed beads, glass
beads, crystals, semiprecious
stones, freshwater pearls,
charms; right angle weave,
spiral rope, wirework
Photo by Shawn Haley

D *Dragon's Tail*, 2012
56 x 1.9 cm
Crystal pearls,
seed beads; netting
Photo by Shawn Haley

THE PIECE CALLED "ANCIENT SEAS" (LEFT) IS A FAVORITE OF MINE, WITH ITS FLOWING DESIGN LINES. ARE YOU MORE COMFORTABLE WITH THIS ORGANIC DESIGN, OR DO YOU BALANCE YOUR WORK WITH STRUCTURE AS WELL?

"Ancient Seas" was an exploration in allowing myself to experience a more organic expression in my beadwork. I tend to bead pieces that are more symmetrical in design while still maintaining a soft, feminine feel. Naturally, I am very proud of what transpired with "Ancient Seas," but in actuality it is not really in my comfort zone.

HOW DO BEADING AND THE INTERNET COME TOGETHER IN YOUR LIFE?

The amazing friends I have made online in the beading community are priceless. Their support, encouragement, understanding, and inspiration are limitless. Sometimes just getting positive feedback from an online friend is all I need to help me finish a project I may be questioning.

"INSPIRATION" IS A COMPELLING WORD. WHERE DOES YOURS COME FROM?

I'm motivated by other beadwork artists, but color is my main inspiration. I will often become distracted when I see a beautiful combination of colors that just happened to land next to each other. Sometimes that distraction is much stronger than my willpower, and I spend the rest of the day creating in my mind.

GIVE ME FOUR WORDS THAT TELL ABOUT YOUR WORK.

Feminine, floral, soft, wearable.

ARE NEW DESIGNS SPONTANE-OUS, OR ARE THEY THE RESULT OF DETAILED PLANNING?

Believe it or not, I get ideas in my dreams! I often wake up with tons of thoughts float-ing in my brain. When one of them is really strong, I'll spend those half-awake hours think-ing through the process of how a design can be created. Other times the beads direct how a piece will turn out—and after all these years I've learned to not argue with the beads.

WHAT DO YOU WANT TO DO WITH YOUR BEADING AS YOU LOOK FORWARD?

Lately I have been playing around a lot with cubic right angle weave. I am most drawn to the simplicity of the stitch rather than a desire to embel-lish it, which is opposite of my usual approach.

WHAT TYPE OF AUDIENCE REAC-TION DO YOU HOPE FOR?

I would be fully content if my viewers just felt happy, from either the form or the colors.

WHAT ARE THE INFLUENCES THAT INFORM YOUR WORK?

I love Art Nouveau and the styles of Mucha, Lalique, and Tiffany. Sometimes just viewing pieces they have created will help me figure out the proper placement or flow of a piece I am working on.

WHAT ARE THE MOST EXCITING MATERIALS YOU WORK WITH?

Seed beads are first and fore-most, followed by sparkling crystals and stones. I also enjoy

A

B

A *Falling Leaves II*, 2011
89 x 5 x 1.3 cm
Cylinder beads, seed beads; diagonal peyote stitch, Rus-sian spiral
Photo by Shawn Haley

B *Magic Blossom*, 2012
8.6 x 3.8 cm
Cylinder beads, seed beads, crystals, crystal pearls; di-agonal peyote stitch, Russian spiral, fringing
Photo by Shawn Haley

C *Nights on Broadway*, 2006
78.7 x 10 x 1.3 cm
Vintage crystals, rivolis, stones, cylinder beads, seed beads, triangle beads; peyote stitch, her-ringbone stitch, embellishment
Photo by Shawn Haley

C

A *Khaleesi*, 2009
61 x 7.6 x 1.3 cm
Pendants, crystal pearls, cylinder beads,
seed beads; peyote stitch, spiral rope
Photo by Shawn Haley

B *The Snake Charmer*, 2012
63 x 14 x 2 cm
Seed beads, stones, beads, pearls; cubic
right angle weave, peyote stitch, netting
Photo by Shawn Haley

C *The Second Season*, 2012
152 x 5 x 1.9 cm
Seed beads, crystal pearls, glass fire-polished beads; right angle weave, fringing
Photo by Shawn Haley

D *Grapevine*, 2006
17.8 x 3.8 cm
Cylinder beads, seed beads, drop beads;
peyote stitch, fringing
Photo by Shawn Haley

A

B

C

Czech glass beads and using small splashes of metal beads such as spacers or drops.

WHAT LEADS YOU TO CHOOSE THE BEADS THAT YOU DO?
I look for quality first, then color, then finish. Aside from that, I let the beads choose me!

WHAT ELSE DO YOU LIKE TO DO TO ENGAGE YOUR ARTISTIC SIDE?
Silversmithing, metal clays, and knitting are some of the other media that I love and have explored in detail. Silversmithing helped teach me the importance of craftsmanship, because errors are not forgiving in metal.

"A solid design sense and a compelling use of color and form draw us to explore the details of Beki's work."
—MARCIA DECOSTER

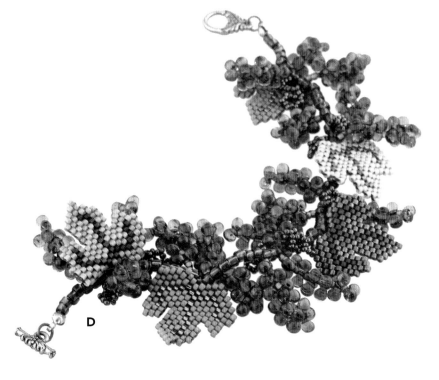

D

betty stephan

"I love making big pieces—that is when I let myself soar. It is a wonderful challenge to use diverse components and techniques in one piece."

I learned to sew at a young age, yet it wasn't until I was in my 50s that I combined this skill with the art of beadwork in the form of bead embroidery. After retiring from my day job in 2005, I became a full-time bead artist. Now I travel throughout the United States exhibiting my intricate pieces at art shows. I've won a number of international awards and contests, and images of my work have been published in *Showcase 500 Beaded Jewelry* (including a cover photo), as well as in *Bead & Button, Beadwork,* and *Ornament* magazines.

bettystephan.com

A

A *Galaxy,* 2012
28 x 27 x 3 cm
Seed beads, felt, adhesive, thread, leather; dimensional bead embroidery
Photo by artist

B *Blue Heaven,* 2011
35 x 20 x 1 cm
Seed beads, polymer clay, picture transfer, stone and glass cabochons, metal findings, crystals, chain, glass beads, stone beads, copper beads, crystal beads, sterling silver wire, adhesive, thread, leather, felt; bead embroidery, right angle weave, peyote stitch, netting stitch
Photo by Tim Fuss

B

YOU HAVE A LOT OF LARGE-SCALE PIECES. DO YOU HAVE A PROCESS THAT HELPS SUSTAIN YOU WHILE WORKING ON SUCH PROJECTS?

I can't work from concept to finish on just one project. I usually work on about six pieces simultaneously, for about an hour each. Of course, if I get really involved, especially with a collar, I will work on it much longer. Music, podcasts, and audio books are relaxing and help me stay focused on the sometimes mundane stitching. I find it to be almost meditative. I don't normally push myself to complete a piece; sometimes it gets put away for weeks at a time.

HOW LONG HAVE YOU BEEN WORKING WITH BEADS?

In 2002 my husband and I attended the Crow Fair, a huge pow-wow in Montana. It was really the first time I had seen such intricate beadwork, and I was fascinated. I purchased a variety of seed beads there, not really knowing what I was going to do with them. I was just so attracted; something about these tiny beads really spoke to me. I was hooked and have been beading ever since.

SO I TAKE IT THE WORKS OF NATIVE AMERICAN ARTISTS HAVE HAD A BIG INFLUENCE ON YOU.

Since the experience at the Crow Fair, I have visited many Native American museums. The intricate and exacting workmanship never fails to humble and inspire me.

WHERE DO YOU FIND ADDITIONAL SOURCES OF INSPIRATION?

Sometimes when I walk through an art gallery, a piece will be screaming to find its way into my work. Quite often my inspiration comes from the materials themselves: the colors and patterns in a particular cabochon, or the sparkle of a focal piece. When I am stuck, I may take a walk and pay particular attention to the colors and textures surrounding me. Right now I am sitting outside looking at a beautiful little bush with clusters of bright red berries, and find myself thinking, I could bead that!!

WHAT OTHER MEDIA HAVE INFLUENCED YOUR WORK?

Sewing and embroidery have given me perhaps the most important skill for beading: being able to thread a needle! Also, I have worked in many media, such as calligraphy, paper quilling,

A

B

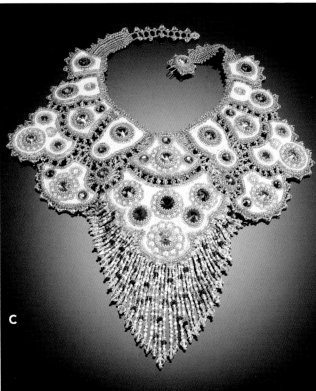

C

A *Guardians*, 2012
33 x 20 x 3 cm
Carved wooden dragons,
smoky quartz crystal, stone and
glass cabochons, crystal points,
seed beads, glass beads, stone
beads, crystal beads, metal
beads, wire, thread, adhesive,
felt, leather; bead embroidery,
peyote stitch
Photo by Tim Fuss

B *Chione*, 2010
36 x 23 x 2 cm
Mother-of-pearl and shell
cabochons, mother-of-pearl
and glass beads, seed beads,
lace, freshwater pearls, shell,
leather, felt, thread, adhesive;
bead embroidery, peyote
stitch, right angle weave
Photo by Tim Fuss

C *Czarina's Puzzle*, 2009
33 x 30 x 1 cm
Seed beads, crystals, adhesive, thread, felt, leather, wire;
bead embroidery, peyote
stitch, herringbone stitch
Photo by Tim Fuss

polymer clay, knitting,
and crochet. All have
helped me develop
indispensible skills,
from recognizing the
importance of negative
space to appreciating
intricate, flowing lines,
to understanding how
small parts come to-
gether to form a whole.

**WHAT ROLE HAS THE
INTERNET PLAYED IN
YOUR BEAD ART?**
Beading is a solitary
occupation most of the
time, so affirmation
from beaders online
always helps if any
self-doubt sneaks into
my mind. Seeing what
others are doing in the
beading world also in-
spires me to try harder
and not fall into a rut.
In addition to present-
ing opportunities for
publishing and com-
petitions, the Internet
makes special materials
easier to source than
ever before.

**WHAT NEW TECH-
NIQUES ARE ON YOUR
MIND?**
I would like to ex-
periment with more
sculptural pieces. I also
want to incorporate
other materials into
my beadwork—spe-
cifically, different kinds
of fibers—and I think
gold-work embroidery
has great potential
to be combined with
beads in jewelry.

HOW DO DIFFERENT MATERIALS INTERACT IN YOUR BEADWORK?

I love working parts of old jewelry into my pieces. I have a huge collection of vintage jewelry, mostly broken or mismatched. I get a lot of satisfaction from working an unwanted or previously loved piece of jewelry into a new design. Stone cabochons also appeal to me. And tiny glass seed beads because of the endless combinations of colors, shapes, sizes, and finishes that make it possible to create three-dimensional pictures.

WHAT DESIGN LESSONS HAVE YOU LEARNED ALONG THE WAY?

I love to quote Jackson Pollock, "The painting has a life of its own, I try to let it come through." I often feel that the design just happens. I don't draw my designs ahead of time, but let the materials guide me. Starting with a main component, I think about what general shape I would like it to be. It is a messy process. I spread out possible components, arrange them on backings, pick a main color and an accent, and start from the center and build.

A

A *Abundance*, 2012
33 x 18 x 2 cm
Seed beads, vintage metal leaf pin, agate druzy cabochon, carved stone leaves, felt, adhesive, thread, leather, wire; bead embroidery, peyote stitch
Photo by Tim Fuss

B *Royal Wedding*, 2012
23 x 18 x 1 cm
Mother-of-pearl cabochons and carving, glass and freshwater pearls, crystals, gold-plated clasp, adhesive, thread, felt, leather; bead embroidery, netting stitch, peyote stitch
Photo by artist

C *Tapestry*, 2011
33 x 16 x 1 cm
Stone cabochons, carved flowers, glass and stone beads, felt, leather, thread, adhesive; bead embroidery, peyote stitch
Photo by artist

D *Rusted Root*, 2011
28 x 18 x 1 cm
Stone cabochons, metal findings, miscellaneous stone, acrylic and glass beads and chips, thread, adhesive, leather, felt; bead embroidery, peyote stitch
Photo by Tim Fuss

HOW DO YOU CHOOSE YOUR BEADS?

It is important for the beads and components to last without fading or breaking. That doesn't necessarily mean they are expensive. I once read that the Art Nouveau period was the first time materials were chosen for the way they looked rather than for their intrinsic value. I agree with this philosophy. A portion of broken costume jewelry might give a piece the overall feeling I am looking for, even better than a diamond would.

"Betty brings a sense of drama and wonder to her elaborately beaded collars."

—MARCIA DECOSTER

siân nolan

I live on the south coast of England with my husband of 25 years, Tony, and our two teenage sons, Toby and Barnaby. I've had a love of craftwork from a young age. My work has been published in *Perlen Poesie* and *The Beadworkers Guild Journal*. I'm also a regular contributor to *UK Bead Magazine*, and I teach in the UK and Germany. My accolades include the Members' Choice Award in the "Eastern Connections" Beadworkers Guild Annual Challenge (2008), and the Experienced Category of the "Treasure Chest Challenge" (2012), sponsored by Swarovski Elements and organized by StitchnCraft Beads.

etsy.com/shop/SianNolan

A

"Vibrant color is at the heart of my work. I continually notice different natural color combinations all around me, and they greatly influence my bead selections."

A *Popsicle Polaris*, 2012
116 x 5 cm
Acrylic beads, seed beads,
crystals, chain; peyote stitch,
right angle weave
Photo by Heather Kingsley-Heath

B *Siâny Bird*, 2012
175 cm
Cylinder beads, crystals, felt,
feathers; peyote, right
angle weave
Photo by Heather Kingsley-Heath

YOU USE SUCH BEAUTIFUL, BRIGHT, JOYOUS COLORS! DO YOU HAVE A SECRET FOR COMBINING THEM INTO PLEASING COMBINATIONS?
There is no secret to my selection of color. I mix, match, and change color combinations frequently until I instinctively feel that I have achieved a near perfect marriage, something that makes me smile! I love bright colors, whether in trinkets, clothes, or beads.

DO YOU HAVE A GOAL IN MIND WHEN YOU SIT DOWN TO START A NEW WORK?
I aspire to create pieces that incorporate a sense of fun, while being colorful, whimsical, cute, and above all, wearable.

WHAT ABOUT A PHILOSOPHY TO GUIDE YOU AS YOU DEVELOP DESIGNS?
I have to confess, designing is something that does not come easy to me. As a self-confessed perfectionist, I am always worried that my ideas won't work. Rachel Nelson Smith says, "Let go of the fear of making a mistake." So once I learned to do that, I was liberated!

DOES THE INTERNET PLAY A ROLE IN YOUR BEAD ART?
I find the Internet is pivotal and indispensable to the success of my beadwork, whether I use it to order beads and materials, perform research, exchange ideas and chat with beading friends using Facebook, or display my designs on Flickr. In fact, my iPad rarely leaves my side.

In addition, I have made many wonderful friends around the world. Undoubtedly, the biggest influence has been the special relationship I have formed with my "bead sister," Petra Tismer (see page 92). She simply oozes enthusiasm and opened a new path in my beading journey by encouraging me to travel to Germany and try my hand at teaching and, most fun of all, plan my first trip to the Bead & Button Show.

WHERE DO YOUR IDEAS COME FROM?

In addition to jewelry and fashion photography, I have a keen interest in Japanese culture and textiles, which is reflected in some of my pieces that include miniature kimono dresses and Japanese-inspired needle cases. I also really love the Japanese trend of kawaii, because it is full of bright colors and cute designs.

DO YOU HAVE A "GETTING STARTED" METHOD?

I find it helpful when starting a new project to choose a huge variety of beads from my stash and put them on a tray. I gradually whittle them down until I am happy with a selected group. Color and finish usually dominate my final choice.

A *Emiko Needle Case*, 2012
8.5 x 2 cm
Wooden form, cylinder beads, crystals, polymer clay; peyote stitch, right angle weave
Photo by Heather Kingsley-Heath

B *Matryoshka Needle Case, Pendant, and Annushka Scissor Charm*, 2011
Needle case: 10 x 2 cm;
Pendant: 8 x 4.5 cm;
Scissor charm: 3 cm
Wooden form, cylinder beads, crystals, hand-painted face; peyote stitch
Photo by Heather Kingsley-Heath

C

C & D *Mermaid's Lagoon*,
2012
18 x 9 x 6 cm
Brass cuff, wooden mermaid,
seed beads, crystals;
bead embroidery
Photos by Heather Kingsley-Heath

D *Spike Cuff*, 2012
7 x 9 x 3 cm
Brass cuff, seed beads, pearls,
spikes, crystals; right
angle weave
Photo by Heather Kingsley-Heath

D

E

WHAT EMOTIONS WOULD YOU LIKE YOUR WORK TO EVOKE?

A sense of fun and inspiration, an appreciation of beautiful color combinations, and a desire to make a similar creation.

WHICH BEAD TECHNIQUES HAVEN'T YOU USED BUT WANT TO?

Well, I can't believe I have never beaded a Cellini spiral, so that surely must top my list! I would also like to learn wirework techniques so I can incorporate more of those into my work.

IS YOUR PRIMARY FOCUS ON JEWELRY, OR DO YOU ENJOY ADDITIONAL FORMS OF BEADWORK?

I love to design cute needle cases and complementing scissor charms. I also own a huge library of Japanese beading books, and I have learned how to make three-dimensional crystal objects. I love the way Japanese designs incorporate detail into such small items, be they handbags, dresses, animals, or characters. The attention to detail is always faultless.

A

B

A *Treasures of the Deep,* 2011
144 cm
Seed beads, crystals, acrylic beads, shells, chain; peyote stitch, right angle weave
Photo by Heather Kingsley-Heath

B *Empress Cixi's Jewel & Emperor XiangFeng's Jewel,* 2011
Empress necklace: 44 cm; Pendant: 7 x 7 cm; Emperor jewel: 32 x 4 cm
24-karat gold-plated seed beads, crystal rondelles, cinnabar beads, crystals; right angle weave, cubic right angle weave
Photo by Heather Kingsley-Heath

C

C *Takara Bangle*, 2011
8 cm
Crystals, pearls; right
angle weave
Photo by Heather Kingsley-Heath

**WHICH MATERIALS ARE
YOUR FAVORITES FOR
BEADWORK?**
That is easy! Swarovski
Crystal Elements, the
sparklier the better, and
Japanese seed beads.
Recently, I have been
incorporating a lot of
Swarovski rose montées
into my designs.

**IN ADDITION TO BEADS,
ARE THERE OTHER
MEDIA YOU ENJOY?**
Prior to beading,
I knitted, cross-
stitched, and was an
enthusiastic bobbin
lacemaker for a few
years. My cross-stitch
and lacemaking skills
have been invaluable,
seamlessly transferring
to beadweaving, which
requires dexterity,
patience, and attention
to detail.

"Vibrant color and a
sense of playfulness
are characteristics
that work seamlessly
together in Siân's fan-
ciful beadwork."
—MARCIA DECOSTER

A

debi keir-nicholson

Simply stated, I am passionate about beads. I have traveled the globe researching and buying beads for my store, Beads of Colour. In pursuit of a degree in interior design, I moved from a small mining community in northern Ontario to "the big city"—Toronto. I subsequently resettled in Dundas, Ontario, where I have built an incredible life with my husband and two boys. My family now includes a treasure trove of bead artists who are customers as well as friends.

beadsofcolour.com

B

A *Honeybunch*, 2011
9 x 9 x 1.3 cm
Vintage plastic beads; right angle weave
Photo by Paul Simon

B *Sporadic Cuff*, 2012
10 x 4.5 x 1.3 cm
Copper-plated beads and seed beads; right angle weave, square stitch
Photo by Paul Simon

C *Pagoda*, designed 2003, rebeaded 2012
Pendant, 15 x 2.5 cm
Seed beads, thread, polymer beads; peyote stitch, Ndebele stitch
Photo by Paul Simon

c

"I am thrilled that at 60 years of age, my inner child is alive and well and I still treasure play days. If I could change one thing about myself, it would be to take life less seriously. I am sure my essence is most apparent when I am having fun or just relaxing."

YOUR USE OF COLOR IS WONDERFUL, ALONG WITH THE ETHNICITY YOUR PIECES SEEM TO EXHIBIT. DO YOU ATTRIBUTE THIS TO ANYTHING IN PARTICULAR?

I love color. In my first year of university, a professor suggested I was "afraid of it," and it has become a passion ever since. When I choose my color palettes, I just let them play with each other and I watch and see how well they get along. This intuitive and intimate approach translates into a more individual expression.

WHY DO YOU LIKE TO MAKE BEADED JEWELRY?

The medium takes me to a quiet place of reflection. The repetition and the assembling of fragments into a whole piece are the reasons this inner atmosphere is created. My pieces are for me. I have mixed emotions when they grow up and leave home: pride, sadness, concern, and excitement. To share them with others has been difficult and yet transforming.

WHAT TYPES OF THINGS INSPIRE YOU IN YOUR WORK?

Fortunately (and sometimes unfortunately), I am stimulated by a wide spectrum of different things, among them are the decaying of a leaf on the beach, the color of a bead and the way it talks to the one beside it, a new technique or a new tool, and a customer's design journey. Inspiration comes easily. It is the discipline of focusing on one idea at a time that is more difficult for me.

WHAT ABOUT IDEAS FOR NEW DESIGNS—WHERE DO THEY COME FROM?

An idea can occur at any time, and is quickly jotted down in one of my many black journals. Some arrive with a mission or in answer to a question or request. Others are more transformational; they pull me down a path just far enough to discover something else that I couldn't see from where I was standing. The physical evolution takes many forms: visualization, sketching, making samples, or talking with other artists or friends.

IN WHAT WAYS DOES THE INTERNET PLAY A ROLE IN YOUR BEAD ART?

The Internet is magical and mysterious. I started a blog to keep in touch with local bead artists who can't get to my store on a regular basis. It has blossomed into a connection with the international bead community. The opportunity to ask questions of so many knowledgeable people is inspiring.

DO YOU LOOK TO OTHER ARTISTIC PURSUITS FOR INSPIRATION?

I spend a great deal of time with my camera. I find that looking through the lens and framing shots gets me out of my head and into a wordless inner realm. From that inner space, everything is possible!

A

B

A *Button Up*, 2012
23 x 2.5 x 0.5 cm
Seed beads, metal buttons, resin rings; free-form peyote stitch
Photo by Paul Simon

B *Hinged Bracelet*, 2006
20 x 6.5 cm
Belt loops, seed beads, thread; peyote stitch
Photo by Paul Simon

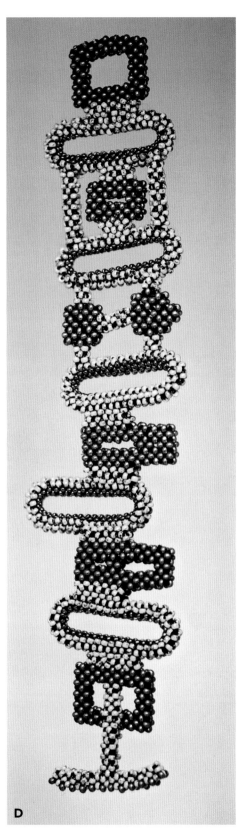

C *Triangle Bracelet*, 2005
20 x 4 cm
Cylinder beads; peyote stitch
Photo by Paul Simon

D *Organically RAW*, 2011
20 x 6.5 cm
Seed beads, metal belt loops,
metal beads; right angle weave
Photo by Paul Simon

WHICH AREAS WITHIN THE BEADING WORLD DO YOU WANT TO DEVELOP FURTHER?

I am in the middle of experiencing one of those rare full-circle moments that is so reaffirming in life. Some of the first pieces I ever produced reflected my love of the natural world and included found objects. The natural world elements seem to be resurfacing in my work. Blending this love with the seed bead knowledge I have acquired is an intoxicating proposition.

DESCRIBE THE EFFECTS YOU WOULD LIKE YOUR JEWELRY TO HAVE ON PEOPLE.

I consider a piece to be extremely successful if I stand a little taller when I put it on and I feel a little more courageous. It would be amazing if I could raise that in others. I once read on someone's blog, "Life is too short to wear department store jewelry." That hits the nail on the head. Get out there, feel good about yourself, and have fun.

"Saturated color, quirky design, and eclectic components all come together in Debi's work, inviting you to explore her intriguing shapes."

—MARCIA DECOSTER

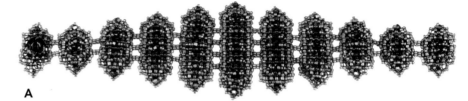

A

nancy dale

I live in southern Vermont with my husband and three dogs, where I am inspired daily by the surrounding countryside. I have been working with beads for 25 years. My main focus has always been seed beads, and the diversity they offer. I am a self-taught beader, which means that all of the truly fabulous and talented artists who went before have showed me the way in their books and magazine articles. I recently took the plunge into writing instructions so that others can make my designs.

nedbeads.com

"As long as one of my bead pieces evokes an emotion, I think I managed to do what I was aiming for."

B

C

A *Draconia Bracelet*, 2010
19 cm
Seed beads, cylinder beads,
crystals; layered right
angle weave
Photo by Sherwood Lake
Photography

B *Sugarplum Purse*, 2011
Purse: 12.7 x 17.8 x 1.27 cm;
Chain: 121.9 cm
Seed beads, metal and crystal clasp, stone cabochon on
reverse side, crystals, synthetic
suede, polyethylene thread;
bead embroidery, peyote stitch,
brick stitch, right angle weave
Photo by Sherwood Lake
Photography

C *Winter Flowers*, 2010
Necklace: 45.7 cm,
Centerpiece: 15.2 cm
Seed beads, freshwater pearls,
crystals, polyethylene thread,
sterling silver jump rings; free-
form right angle weave, right
angle weave, peyote
stitch, fringing
Photo by Sherwood Lake
Photography

YOU DO BEAUTIFUL FRINGE—ANY SECRETS TO SHARE?

Thank you! Fringe should always be of interest, but it should flow and complete the piece without compet-ing for attention with the focal. I try to gather beads that speak to the rest of the piece. Fringe can be over-planned— it looks best when it is a natural extension of your piece. Plac-ing end beads on the mat under the work and judging its length from there makes the process much easier than stringing several strands and then hav-ing to undo them if they look wrong.

WHAT WORD DESCRIBES YOUR WORK?

Intuitive. I bead from the heart, and follow what feels right, rather than following strict rules of beading. I love the "what if" part of creating with beads!

HOW LONG HAVE BEADS BEEN YOUR MEDIUM FOR CREATING ART?

I started with a pair of brick-stitched earrings a quarter century ago and have never looked back.

DID YOU START WITH JEWELRY AS THE ME-DIUM TO SATISFY YOUR ARTISTIC SPIRIT?

I've written fiction, drawn using pencil and ink, and crocheted.

I think all of these led me to beadwork—I had to find what I was not passionate about before I found my true inspiration and passion in beading. Beadwork is the medium that has allowed me to transform my vision into tangible reality.

HOW DOES THE INTERNET PLAY A ROLE IN YOUR BEAD ART? HAVE ONLINE RELATIONSHIPS CHANGED YOUR WORK IN ANY WAY?

As a shy person, I have never made friends easily. The Internet provides that little bit of space that makes it easier to meet people, and easier to be a little more relaxed with who I am.

I have had the incredible good fortune to meet many of my artistic heroines (and heroes!) through social media, and they have influenced me hugely in how I now look at beading as an art form, and how to relate to people through that art form. I would not have gotten as far as I have in exploring the world of beads without the support and encouragement of several very special online friends and artists. I have no words for how grateful I am to each of them.

WHAT INSPIRES YOU?

Almost everything I make is inspired by nature—perhaps the view out my window, a walk in the woods, or the stone cabochon I'm working with—although fantasy

A

A *Galaxy*, 2011
Centerpiece: 17.8 cm; Necklace: 45.7 cm
Seed beads, freshwater pearls, crystals, dichroic glass cabochons, amethyst, onyx, various natural stone beads and cabochons, sterling silver, copper, synthetic suede, base metal centerpiece; bead embroidery, peyote stitch, fringing
Photo by Sherwood Lake Photography

B *Dancer Earrings*, 2012
6.4 x 3.1 cm
Seed beads, crystals, cubic zirconia drops, polymer clay cabochons by Mary Marshall, copper, synthetic suede, polyethylene thread; bead embroidery, brick stitch, peyote stitch, fringing
Photo by Sherwood Lake Photography

B

C

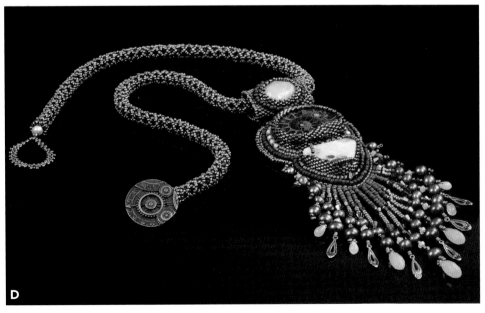

D

C *Reflections*, 2012
50.8 cm
Seed beads, bugle beads, cube beads, freshwater pearls, crystals, pressed-glass beads, assorted natural semiprecious stone beads, labor-dorite cabochons, emeralds, copper, polyethylene thread, synthetic suede; free-form peyote stitch, free-form right angle weave, tubular and flat peyote stitches, fringing, improvisational stitching, brick stitch, bead embroidery
Photo by Sherwood Lake Photography

D *Horn of Ammon*, 2011
50.8 cm
Seed beads, base metal button, base metal charms, ammonite fossil, opal cabochon, crystals, freshwater pearls, pressed-glass drops, synthetic suede, polyethylene thread; bead embroi-dery, peyote stitch, brick stitch, right angle weave, netting
Photo by Sherwood Lake Photography

and science fiction play a role as well. I love trees and the mythology that surrounds them, and I like to include a bit of tree in almost everything.

WHAT IS YOUR PLANNING PROCESS FOR CREATING DESIGNS?

I rarely plan, and if I do, the project always takes a turn away from what I had in mind. An idea usually starts as a vague picture in my head, and then becomes whatever it will—or whatever it won't, as the case may be. The way I know if an idea will work is to try it.

IS JEWELRY YOUR MAIN FOCUS OF BEADWORK, OR ARE THERE ADDITIONAL FORMS YOU ALSO LIKE?

My focus shifts from year to year. I have sculptural works, beaded rocks, vessels, and purses in my beady room, but this past year has been all about jewelry.

WHAT DO YOU WANT TO DO WITH YOUR BEADWORK THAT YOU HAVEN'T FULLY INVESTIGATED YET?

I plan on exploring bead embroidery more, and I love seeing what can be achieved with right angle weave. I would also like to work more on sculptural or interpretive pieces. Free-form beadwork is comfortable for me, and I have a lot of fun with the process. Finally, I find myself drawn to fibers, but haven't yet come up

A

B

C

A *Juliet Necklace*, 2012
50.8 x 6.3 cm
Seed beads, freshwater pearls, crystals, polyethylene thread; right angle weave, peyote stitch
Photo by Sherwood Lake Photography

B *Juliet Bracelet*, 2010 (component detail)
7.6 x 3.8 (each component)
Seed beads, freshwater pearls, crystals, polyethylene thread; right angle weave, peyote stitch
Photo by Sherwood Lake Photography

C *Faux Lariat*, 2012
114.3 x 2.5 cm
Seed beads, cylinder beads, freshwater pearls, bugle beads, chain, jump rings, brass beads, crystals, pearl beads, brass washers, keys, polyethylene thread; tubular hexagonal right angle weave, fringing, wirework
Photo by Sherwood Lake Photography

with a satisfying way to combine them with my beadwork.

WHAT FEELINGS WOULD YOU LIKE TO EVOKE IN THOSE WHO SEE YOUR WORK?
I want viewers to be inspired in some way, whether to pick up beads and make something themselves, or to touch or wear the piece they're viewing. I want the viewer to feel what I was feeling during the piece's creation, even if it was sad or angry.

HOW DO YOU CHOOSE THE BEADS YOU USE?
I gather a huge pile of beads, all different sizes and shapes, in the colors I have chosen for my project, and then whittle it down to the ones I will use as I work with my focal. Texture is important, and then I see which pearl looks good, or which crystal might look better in its place.

"Nancy's masterful capturing of cabochons enhances their natural beauty as she adds just the right colors and design elements to highlight the stones' qualities."

—**MARCIA DECOSTER**

D *Dryad*, 2010
50.8 cm
Seed beads, freshwater pearls, crystals, pressed-glass beads, assorted natural semiprecious stone beads, polymer clay cabochons created by Chris Kapano of Mandarin Moon, dichroic glass cabochons, synthetic suede, polyethylene thread; bead embroidery, peyote stitch, fringing, right angle weave, improvisational stitching, brick stitch
Photo by Sherwood Lake Photography

E *Calliope Bracelet*, 2012
17.8 x 2.5 x 2.5 cm
Seed beads, spike beads, crystals, polyethylene thread; peyote stitch, modified right angle weave
Photo by Sherwood Lake Photography

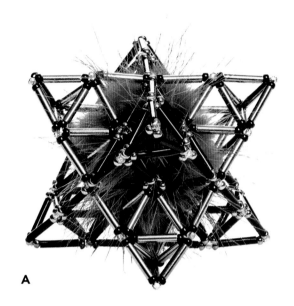

A

martina nagele

"Beads make my life a bit 'sparklier' and happier, and I hope my beadwork can pass this sparkle on to others."

Growing up in Bavaria, I explored a number of needlework techniques throughout my youth. Then in 2006 I discovered beads. Beads? BEADS!! It was like someone had opened a door to a new, exciting, sparkling world. Today I live near Bonn, a crystallization point of the German beading scene. From 2010 to 2012, I served as technical editor and translator for *Perlen Poesie* magazine. I have offered beading work-shops at the BeadArt Fair in Hamburg and taught classes at several Bead & Button shows.

mariposa8000.blogspot.de

B

C

A *Drag! Me! Out!*, 2012
5 x 5 x 5 cm
Seed beads, bugle beads, crystals,
fur; right angle weave variation
Photo by Christian Daitche/FOTOBONN

B *Antarctica*, 2012
18 x 2 cm
Lampworked drops by Uli Kreit-
erling, seed beads, fire-polished
beads; right angle weave
Photo by Christian Daitche/FOTOBONN

C *Jeannie in a Bottle*, 2012
8 x 2 x 2 cm
Vintage glass drop, seed beads,
chain; herringbone stitch, netting
Photo by Christian Daitche/FOTOBONN

MUCH OF YOUR WORK HAS A WHIMSICAL SENSE. HOW DO YOU DREAM UP SUCH FANCIFUL CREATIONS?

Maybe deep inside me there is still a child (a quite childish child, I suppose) and I wonder if she sometimes knocks on the inside of my head. I love to throw in unexpected, surprising ingredients that provoke a second look.

AND WHAT DO YOU THINK STIRS THAT INNER CHILD INTO ARTISTIC ACTION?

Hmmm … where to start? A piece of art, a fabric pattern, a song, a book cover, a newspaper headline, a movie, flowers, a color combo … it could be almost anything. I once took a picture of a lovely scroll pattern on a cookie (for the record, it was a double vanilla wafer with coconut cream).

ABOUT THE TYPE OF BEADWORK YOU DO—HOW WOULD YOU CHARACTERIZE IT?

Square. Sober. Straightforward. No ruffles. No fringes. Like me. And then I'm suddenly struck by those severe embellishment and whimsy attacks …

HOW DO YOU WORK YOUR DESIGN PROCESS?

I don't usually have the time to test an idea when it first pops into my head. So I put my thoughts into the "ideas" folder on my computer as soon as I can. Then the idea can percolate for days or even weeks. It is important to know beads and how different sizes and shapes behave with different stitches. Then I can predict which beads will provide the results I want while avoiding mistakes. By the time I pick up thread, needle, and the first bag of beads, the design has often already taken shape in my mind.

HOW DO YOU USE THE INTERNET IN YOUR BEADING WORLD?

I can no longer imagine my crafting life without it. As much as I love to socialize and shop in my local bead shop, blogging and social media (and Skyping) are wonderful opportunities to get in contact with beaders from all over the globe. The Internet is a never-ending source of inspiration because the interaction with an international group of artists who share the same interest is exciting and motivating.

DESCRIBE SOME OF THE RELATIONSHIPS YOU'VE DEVELOPED ONLINE AND HOW THEY INFLUENCE YOU.

I joined Facebook to connect with my beading idols, so I could maybe stalk them one day at a show and scream, "Hey, I am your FB buddy!" To my surprise, those celebrities were all lovely people and that scenario was suddenly something that could really happen! Yay!!

A

B

C

Over time my contact with some of these people got quite close. We all enjoy our online meet-and-bead sessions where we ask one another for help on technical problems, share design secrets, and trade recipes for candied pecans.

WHICH BEAD TECHNIQUES WOULD YOU LIKE TO EXPLORE IN FUTURE WORK?
I'd like to combine classic off-loom beading with other techniques like chain mail or wirework. And I want to try my hand at bead embroidery.

HOW DO YOU CHOOSE THE BEADS YOU USE?
I use the best-quality materials I can afford. It takes many, many hours to complete a beaded work of art. So it deserves even-sized and colorfast beads, the most sparkling of crystals, non-breaking threads, and good-quality findings.

"Martina's sense of humor coupled with her technical competence make for innovative beadwork. Pink fur balls inside of structures and cows grazing on grass are just two examples of very fun work."

—MARCIA DECOSTER

A & B *Elsa in the Rough,* 2012
18 x 2.5 cm
Seed beads, crystals, artificial grass, resin; right angle weave
Photos by Christian Daitche/ FOTOBONN

C *Estelle, Spherical Studies,* 2012
4 cm and 6 cm (diameters)
Seed beads, bugle beads, pearls, crystals; right angle weave variation
Photo by Christian Daitche/ FOTOBONN

D *Squirrel's Bouquet,* 2010
5 x 3 x 2 cm
Seed beads, crystals, keshi pearls, copper beads; herring-bone stitch, fringing
Photo by Christian Daitche/ FOTOBONN

A

B

helena tang-lim

Inspired by a pair of antique Straits Chinese beaded shoes, I set out to learn the art of bead tapestry so I could make a similar pair. From then on, beading became an all-consuming passion. My beadwork features many elements of my ethnic Chinese culture as well as influences from the rich potpourri of colors and images of Southeast Asia. Retired from corporate life, I currently live in sunny Singapore and design and sell my beadwork jewelry, kits, and patterns online at Manek-Manek Beads.

manek-manek.com

A *Viking Queen*, 2012
Ropes: 50 cm,
Pendants: 6.5 x 5.5 cm
Seed beads, glass spikes, crystals; peyote stitch, herringbone stitch
Photo by Eric Lim

B *Collier Joséphine*, 2012
50 cm
Seed beads, crystal pearls, twin beads, glass spikes; peyote stitch
Photo by Eric Lim

C *La Collana Dei Medici*, 2012
42 cm
Seed beads, crystals, cubic zirconia pendant, drop beads; modified lattice weave, right angle weave, herringbone stitch
Photo by Eric Lim

c

"I would like my audience to feel wonder—wonder that tiny bits of colored glass can be woven to have form and be used to create works of beauty."

YOU SEEM TO HAVE FUN PLAYING WITH SPIKES. ARE THERE CHALLENGES WHEN DESIGNING SUCH A UNIQUE COMPONENT?

Rightly or wrongly, spikes conjure images of Goth and the dark arts for me, and my style is so very far from those. But I find spikes fascinating, so challenge number one is to make them elegant. Through their colors and their roles as focal beads or as large beads, spikes have become part of the landscape of my bead-weaving rather than elements that jar the harmony of a piece. And challenge number two is more technical, because spikes generally have a hole going through the base. How do I keep them in place so they don't wobble? For this, I sometimes wrap the base in various stitches or weave little nets to hold them in place.

WHICH OTHER MEDIA HAVE YOU USED IN ART OR CRAFT, AND HAVE THEY INFORMED THE WAY YOU WORK NOW?

I have dabbled in knitting, crochet, and cross-stitch em-broidery since I was young. So the knitting and crochet were extremely useful when I started incorporating beads into them.

WHAT ARE YOU AIMING FOR WHEN YOU DESIGN A PIECE?

I like making intricate pieces that are by no means simple in construction and tech-nique. The challenge then is to have the simplicity belie its complexity. Many have described my pieces as elegant, sophisticated but understated, and wearable.

HOW DO YOUR DESIGNS COME TO MIND?

Common, everyday things as well as elements from my ethnic Chinese and Southeast Asian cultures, in addition to inspiration from fellow beaders' pieces, all play large roles in the germination of designs. Because I cannot draw to save my life, my designs generally stay inside my head until completion. Usually, I see the completed piece in my mind's eye, along with its convoluted thread paths, connections, and components. When I finally pick up my needle and beads, the piece is almost completed. Of course, the beads sometimes do not cooperate, and then it's back to my virtual drawing board.

HOW IS THE INTERNET INVOLVED IN YOUR BEAD ART?

Initially, I went online to source the charlottes that I used for my beaded shoes because finding them locally was next to impossible. I also used the Internet to discover how to weave and learn certain techniques. Since then, it has become a major source of inspiration as I discover different styles of beadwork and beaders.

WHICH OTHER ARTISTIC MEDIA EXCITE YOU?

Soutache is my current favorite for inspiration. I love the intricacies created by soutache ribbon. Chinese knotting and button making are also media that I draw inspiration from.

A

B

C

WHICH BEAD TECHNIQUES WOULD YOU LIKE TO EXPLORE IN FUTURE WORK?
I would like to learn lampworking. Unfortunately, there are not many lampworkers in Singapore, so it may be a while yet before I get to try this.

IS JEWELRY YOUR MAIN FOCUS, OR DO YOU WORK WITH ADDITIONAL FORMS OF BEADWORK?
Being a woman, I have a tendency to make articles of jewelry. Generally, I just bead whatever strikes my fancy. I have done Christmas ornaments, Easter eggs, Malay ketupat (glutinous rice wrapped in leaves and cooked), and, of course, my beaded shoes.

DO YOU FIND YOURSELF RETURNING TO CERTAIN TYPES OF BEADS TIME AND AGAIN?
I cannot resist tiny, precious, metal-plated glass beads. And crystals—the more bling the better. I also find myself attracted to unusual things such as beetle wings, glass eyes, and spikes.

"Understated elegance and superb workmanship are the hallmarks of Helena's lovely and infinitely wearable designs."

—MARCIA DECOSTER

A *Snowflake*, 2012
9.5 x 9.5 cm
Seed beads, glass spikes, crystals; cubic right angle weave
Photo by Eric Lim

B & C *Maharani*, 2012
52 cm
Seed beads, crystals, grosgrain ribbon, synthetic suede; bead embroidery, peyote stitch, modified right angle weave
Photos by Eric Lim

D *Aztec Princess Collar*, 2012
Necklace: 45 cm;
Pendant: 10.5 x 5.8 cm
Seed beads, crystals, two-hole tile beads, polymer clay cabochon by Agi Kiss (Moonsafari Beads), synthetic suede; bead embroidery, peyote stitch, stringing
Photo by Eric Lim

E *Longevity & Love*, 2012
56 cm
Seed beads, crystal pearls, howlite butterfly; cubic right angle weave
Photo by Eric Lim

heather kingsley-heath

Following a career in design and magazine editorial, I began beading as a curiosity, but it quickly became my passion after taking a day class with Sue Jackson and Wendy Hubrick. I am the creative force behind albion stitch, a new beading technique about which I've written several books. I live and work in Somerset, England, and my work has been featured in *Perlen Poesie*, *Beadwork*, *Bead*, and many other magazines. I teach in the UK and overseas, publish books, kits and patterns, and create pieces to commission.

heatherworks.co.uk

www.albionstitch.com

"Storytelling is at the heart of everything I make: the story I tell myself to get started, the one that emerges once the process is underway, and the story other people interpret when they see a finished piece."

A

A *Cute Bird Charms*, 2012
4 x 4 x 3 cm each
Seed beads, mini droplet
beads; albion stitch
Photo by artist

B *Little Owl Charms*, 2011
7 x 4 x 3 cm each
Seed beads, crystal pearls,
wool fleece stuffing, wire,
phone charm strap; albion
stitch, peyote stitch, brick
stitch, ladder stitch, right
angle weave, netting
Photo by artist

C *Beaded Beetle and
Beaded Butterfly*, 2010;
Flowers and Leaves, 2009
Beetle brooch: 6.5 x 6 x 1.5 cm;
Butterfly brooch: 6 x 7 x 1 cm;
Flowers and leaves:
15 x 12 x 8 cm
Beetle: Crystal stones, crystals,
seed beads, cylinder beads;
albion stitch, peyote stitch
Butterfly: Crystals, seed beads,
cylinder beads, wire, brooch
pin; albion stitch, peyote
stitch, wirework
Flower and leaves: Silk,
embroidery thread, wire, fabric
dye; hand stitched
Photo by artist

WHEN DID YOU START BEADING?
I remember playing with a piece of string and Grandma's button box, and haven't stopped since. But I began beading as a creative art form about 15 years ago, with the pure luxury of working with beads full time for the past two.

I LOVE THE CUTE FACTOR OF YOUR BEADED OWLS AND BIRDS. HOW DO YOU GO ABOUT CREATING THE REALISM IN AN OBJECT?
I really enjoy the challenge; it's fun to sum up shapes with beads and stitches. It's not so much about creating exact replicas; it's more about how a collection of shapes can suggest things. The cute factor is random, and it usually arrives just when I think I'm being a "serious artist."

DO YOU HAVE A GOAL WHEN YOU SET ABOUT TO CREATE A PIECE OF BEADED ART?
I usually have a story in mind. Recent designs include hidden spaces to contain a personal treasure, votive, prayer, or wish. I like to combine a wide range of seed beading techniques in the figurative pieces. I aim for delicate but interestingly textured shapes. For me, creating structure is the best fun to explore.

WHERE DOES INSPIRATION ORIGINATE?

Where to start? Texture and color, a mood, a snippet of music, something I see in the garden or while traveling. From there, a story begins to take shape in my head about how these ideas could be translated into beads, and why. Sometimes answering the "why" part is the most inspiring bit.

WHAT EFFECTS DO YOU HOPE TO ACHIEVE IN YOUR VIEWERS?

I want to invoke a sense of intrigue and a desire to possess, as in, "How does she do that? I have so got to make me one of those!" Which is why my online logo reads, "See Love Bead Wear."

HOW DO YOUR DESIGNS COME ABOUT?

I doodle, then I gather beads. Spreading the bead piles onto a mat is a magical time of hope and promise. After selecting beads, I spend many hours executing millions of rip-outs and start-overs, loving every curiosity-inspired, frustrating minute of it!

HOW DO YOU CHOOSE YOUR BEADS FOR A PIECE?

With hunger, lust, and passion.

HOW HAVE BLOGS INFLUENCED YOU?

Blogs are a place where a beader can set out his or her stall and dialogue about things. The best blogs draw me in with a warm personality—a sureness about what creates simple joy. It took me a long time to pluck up the courage, but now I blog and I love it as a medium of self-expression.

A

A *Land of Oleander Tassel,* 2009
Tassel: 65 x 9 x 9 cm;
Bird: 12 x 11 x 4 cm;
Stick: 68 x 1 x 5 cm;
Tassel: Wooden bead armature, seed beads, crystals; herringbone stitch, albion stitch, ladder stitch, brick stitch, fringing
Bird: Seed beads, accent beads, felt and wire armature; bead embroidery
Stick: Wooden base, hand-dyed silk yarn, seed beads, textile, wire; seed bead embroidery, netting
Photo by artist

B *Bella Pendant (top), Indiaman Pendant (bottom),* 2011 both pieces
Bella: 7 x 2 x 2 cm;
Indiaman: 8.5 x 3.5 x 2.5 cm
Bella: Seed beads, crystal chaton, pearls; peyote stitch, ladder stitch, herringbone stitch, netting
Indiaman: Seed beads, crystal rivoli, glass pearls, crystals; albion stitch, netting
Photo by artist

B

D

E

C *Wave Bead Necklace,* 2010
Necklace: 54 cm;
Large bead: 4 x 3 x 4 cm;
Small wave bead: 3 x 2 x 3 cm
Seed beads, briolette cushion
beads, round glass beads, wire,
metal ring; albion stitch, wire
jewelry-making techniques
Photo by artist

D *The Time Traveler's*
Compass Pendant, 2012
Pendant: 14 x 7 x 2 cm
Seed beads, spike beads, fire-pol-
ished crystals, crystal chaton, glass
pearls, jewelry tube; albion stitch,
honeycomb netting, peyote stitch
Photo by artist

E *Acantha Lariat,* 2012
Central motif: 6 x 4 cm;
End pieces: 4 x 2.5 x 2.5 cm
Seed beads, crystal chaton, fire-
polished crystals, spike beads, glass
pearls, knit cord; albion stitch, netting
Photo by artist

C

**LOOK TO THE FUTURE . . .
WHICH AVENUES WOULD
YOU LIKE TO EXPLORE?**
Albion stitch remains a
huge love affair for me,
with so many possibili-
ties still to investigate.
I am also fascinated by
ways to go from one
technique to another
within a piece. My epic
fail to date, and the one
I would really like to
master, is the art of bead
crochet.

"Heather is an
architect of three-
dimensional pieces,
many of which include
a sense of playfulness;
others are exquisite
necklaces begging to
be worn."

—MARCIA DECOSTER

A

elke
leonhardt-rath

I grew up in Cologne, Germany, learning all types of needlework techniques from my grandmother at a very early age. Knitting, crocheting, and sewing soon became a part of my life. I also enjoyed weaving little beaded bracelets, which was a popular activity in my country during the 1970s.

Today, I live with my family near Bonn. The beading bug bit me in the late '90s. I initially incorporated seed beads into cross-stitch work, and then crocheted many different tubular chains. I subsequently learned all sorts of beadweaving techniques and began to modify templates and patterns to create my own designs. Right angle weave has now become my favorite technique.

"Lots of things inspire me. For example, the variety in nature, such as the shapes and colors of flowers, never ceases to fascinate me. And architectural structures and geometric shapes also influence my work."

B

C

CAN YOU DESCRIBE YOUR BASIC APPROACH TO BEADING?

I often work intuitively. I might find a great rivoli that may sit for weeks before a spark ignites within me. And then I experiment until the result ends up as I envisioned. I will decide whether this becomes a pendant, a bracelet, or a pair of earrings as I work, and I create variants accordingly. Only when I like the result do I decide whether the piece is suitable for a pattern or whether it is to remain as a single, unique item.

HOW DO YOU CHOOSE THE BEADS YOU USE?

I lay out an array of beads for potential use—seed beads in all sizes, charlotte beads, crystals, drops, pearls—whatever I can think of. Many are soon placed back in the cupboard as I work; some are replaced; some new ones are added. I love this creative mess on my table, though I admit I hate having to sort and clean up when the work is completed.

A *Notre Dame,* 2011
19.5 x 4.5 cm
Seed beads, cabochons, crystal bicones; right angle weave, embellishment
Photo by Claudia Schumann

B *Wrapped with Beads,* 2012
20 x 1.5 cm
Leather, round pearls, crystal bicones, cylinder beads, seed beads; peyote stitch, free-form stitches
Photo by Frank Schmole

C *Polaris-Sonne,* 2009
3.5 x 3.5 x 2 cm
Polaris pearl, cylinder beads, seed beads, crystal bicones; peyote stitch
Photo by Frank Schmole

YOU'VE PUBLISHED A BEAUTIFUL BOOK ON RIGHT ANGLE WEAVE AND CUBIC RIGHT ANGLE WEAVE. WHAT ARE THE PROPERTIES YOU FIND APPEALING IN THESE STITCHES?

The amazing thing about right angle weave is the possibility of working in three dimensions. If you combine different sizes and types of beads, you can create virtually any shape you want.

IN WHAT WAYS HAVE ONLINE RELATIONSHIPS AFFECTED YOU?

I'd like to talk about you, Marcia. If it weren't for the Internet, you would never have come to Perlament in Bonn where we met, and I would never have flown to the Bead & Button show to further our relationship. Additionally, we would not share mutual friends from around the world. This has led to my jewelry becoming known in other countries and the opportunity to offer classes to an international audience . . . the list goes on and on!

A

A & B *Der Drache auf dem Vulkan Necklace*, 2012
47 x 6 x 1.5 cm
Seed beads, cabochons, crystal bicones, crystal rounds, polyethylene thread; right angle weave
Photos by Frank Schmole

C *Like Little Drops*, 2010
42 x 1.2 cm
Seed beads, crystals, drop beads, polyethylene thread; right angle weave
Photo by Frank Schmole

B

C

D

E

D *Geometrical Necklace,* 2011
95 x 4 cm
Seed beads, crystal bicones, polyethylene thread; right angle weave, peyote stitch
Photo by Frank Schmole

E *Geometrical Bracelet,* 2011
19 x 3 x 0.5 cm
Seed beads, crystal bicones, magnet clasp, polyethylene thread; right angle weave, peyote stitch
Photo by Frank Schmole

A

B

C

A & B *Rotunde der San Jose City Hall Necklace,* 2011
47 x 2 x 4 cm
Seed beads, round crystals, pearls, thread, jewelry wire, clasp; tubular right angle weave, wirework
Photos by Frank Schmole

C *Seestern,* 2008
7 x 7 x 3.5 cm
Seed beads, cylinder beads, crystal bicones, thread; peyote stitch, fringing
Photo by Frank Schmole

E

F

D Untitled Pendant, 2012
8 x 3 x 3 cm
Seed beads, drop beads, cabochons,
pearls, fine metal chain, polyethylene
thread; peyote stitch
Photo by Frank Schmole

E *Froschteich*, 2012
10 x 5 x 5 cm
Seed beads, cylinder beads, crystals,
cabochon, metal frog, polyethylene thread;
peyote stitch, free form stitch
Photo by Heiko Radermacher

F *Cosmic Capsule*, 2012
6.5 x 4 x 4 cm
Seed beads, crystal bicones, pearls, nylon thread,
polyethylene thread; right angle weave, netting
Photo by Frank Schmole

**WHICH BEAD TECHNIQUES
WOULD YOU LIKE TO
EXPLORE IN FUTURE WORK?**
I like combining different
techniques, such as starting
a border in right angle weave
and continuing with the
peyote stitch. I also really
enjoy combining different
materials, such as felt and
beads or fabric and beads.

**WHICH MATERIALS ARE
YOUR FAVORITES?**
I work most often with
Japanese seed beads; the
smaller, the better. I combine
them with the brilliance and
radiance of Austrian crystals.
I've recently started using
more good-quality Czech
beads that come in unusual
shapes. I place great emphasis
on high-quality clasps,
because the many hours that
go into creating these pieces
should reflect quality.

**HOW DO YOU WANT
OTHERS TO RESPOND TO
YOUR JEWELRY?**
Many of my pieces are
elaborate and therefore
involve a great deal of
work! So I feel highly
complimented when anyone
takes the time to follow my
patterns. I am gratified when
another beader's enthusiasm
goes beyond mere
admiration of my work and
is channeled into creating his
or her own piece.

"Elke's mastery of
cubic right angle weave
gives her work intricate
connections that create
visual complexity."

—MARCIA DECOSTER

Throughout my life in South Africa, crafts have played an important role, and I am blessed with a husband who encourages and supports me. On a visit to the United States in 1998, I stumbled upon a bead shop. The beauty of the beads I saw there lured me to learn more, and I became obsessed with beads. Upon my return home, I started to design my own projects. Eventually, I was able to publish in local and international craft magazines, including *Bead & Button* and *Beadwork*. Seeing a need for would-be beading teachers to receive professional training, I started my very popular Master the Bead Stitch.

rianaolckers.blogspot.com

riana bootha olckers

A

"Beading is part of my being, and I plan to always design patterns to share with other beadweaving enthusiasts."

B

A *Jabulani*, 2012
45 x 3 x 3 cm
Bicones, glass pearls, seed
beads, drop beads, thread;
right angle weave,
peyote stitch
Photo by Paul Machael Olckers

B *Thulani Bracelet*, 2010
20 x 4 x 0.5 cm
Seed beads, tiger-eye faceted
round cabochons, bicones,
thread; peyote stitch, right
angle weave
Photo by Paul Machael Olckers

C *Olga*, 2011
Necklace: 42 x 3.5 cm;
Pendant: 18 x 9 x 3.5 cm
Seed beads, drop
beads, bicones, glass
pearls, rivolis, thread,
jump rings, head pin;
peyote stitch, herring-
bone stitch, right
angle weave
Photo by Paul Machael
Olckers

YOU SEEM DRAWN TO LAYERS OF TEXTURE AND THE RICHNESS OF METALLICS. DO YOU HAVE A FAVORITE SET OF COLORS AND STITCHES?
Copper, bronze, gold, purple, and green are the colors I favor because they give the beadwork an old-world charm. My favorite stitch is peyote stitch with all possible variations I can think of. I also feature herringbone and right angle weave regularly, and I often combine all three in my designs.

YOUR DESIGNS ALSO SEEM SIMPLE—IN A GOOD WAY, OF COURSE. WOULD YOU AGREE WITH THAT OBSERVATION?
I might describe them as minimalist, not too elaborate. I prefer designs that you can wear and not ones that wear you.

WHAT TYPES OF THINGS HAVE INFLUENCED YOUR BEADING?
I find myself inspired by the jewelry worn by the royalty in days gone by, particularly the Indian, Russian, and European royalties.

WHAT ARE YOUR FAVORITE BEADS TO WORK WITH?
Right now they are Japanese and Czech seed beads—all sizes and shapes. Also bicones and pearls.

WHAT ARE YOU THINKING ABOUT AS YOU CHOOSE YOUR BEADS?
Bead choice is dictated by the color phase I am experiencing at that particular moment in time.

HOW DO YOU COME UP WITH DESIGNS?

They just pop into my head. From there, I scribble them down in my black book and write the stitch or stitch combination along with the color and size of beads I think will be appropriate. Then I work up a quick sample. But it may take months or years to come back and finish a particular design. I am known for my "unfinished projects" boxes.

YOU BEGAN BEADING IN 1998. HAS THE GROWTH OF THE INTERNET OFFERED BENEFITS YOU COULDN'T HAVE IMAGINED BACK THEN?

The Internet opened the world to meeting fellow artists and to being inspired by their creations. We can share our art with nearly the whole universe and get immediate feedback; I trust these fellow artists to test my patterns and give honest criticism. South Africa is quite a distance from Europe and America, and even though I love to teach, it is not always possible to travel that far. And the ability to sell my patterns over the Internet gives me the satisfaction of sharing my craft.

A

A *Annah Tiger*, 2012
60 x 1.5 x 1.5 cm
Seed beads, cubes, bicones, top-drilled crystals, glass pearls, magnetic clasp, thread; tubular peyote stitch
Photo by Paul Machael Olckers

B *African Diamonds*, 2007
45 x 4 x 3.5 cm
Seed beads, hexagons, bicones, thread; peyote stitch, herringbone stitch
Photo by Paul Machael Olckers

C *Nuts about You Necklace*, 1999
50 x 5 cm
Seed beads, thread, wooden beads, wire, clasp; herringbone stitch, peyote stitch
Photo by Paul Machael Olckers

D *Nandi's Crown*, 2012
Neckband: 42 x 1.5 cm; Pendant: 3.2 x 7 cm
Seed beads, rubber tube (neckband), thread, hook, clasp; peyote stitch, herringbone stitch
Photo by Paul Machael Olckers

B

C

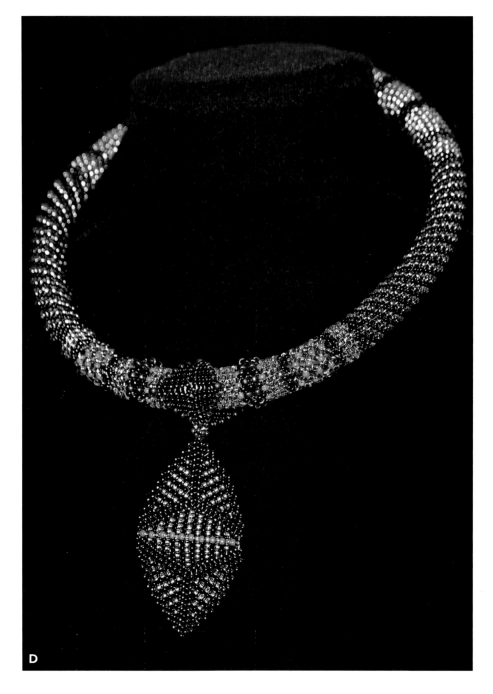

D

HAVE OTHER ARTISTIC MEDIA INFORMED YOUR WORK?
Yes. I'd say that stained glass soldering and pewter repoussé art have influenced me to produce beadwork in three dimensions and to create texture.

ARE YOU CURRENTLY WORKING ON ANY NEW TECHNIQUES?
Yes, I'm presently trying to master the chevron stitch.

DO YOU LIKE TO MAKE BEAD CREATIONS THAT ARE NOT JEWELRY?
My main focus is jewelry, but I also enjoy creating Christmas ornaments.

WHAT REACTION DO YOU WANT YOUR WORK TO IN-SPIRE IN OTHERS?
I would like people to look at any one of my designs and say, "I want to make and wear this myself!"

"Riana's colors and use of materials invoke an ethnic feel to the jewelry she creates."
—MARCIA DECOSTER

cynthia newcomer daniel

My grandmothers and my parents were my first teachers, so I have been beading and making jewelry for nearly 50 years. I also enjoy creating with textiles, fibers, and precious metals—it is wonderful to experiment and adapt techniques from one medium to another. I find much of my beading inspiration in my California countryside, where I am surrounded by golden hills, blue skies, and the rich colors of vineyards.

jewelrytales.com

"Beads continually surprise me; every day it seems as if I find something new that can be done with them."

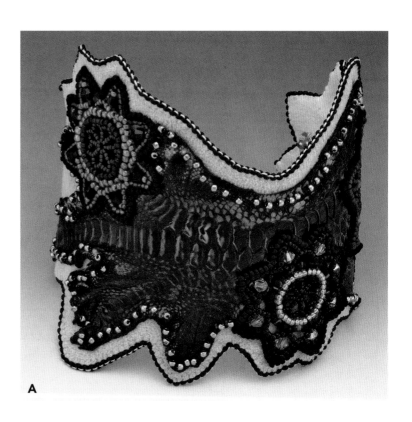

A

B

A *Chicken Foot*, 2011
21.5 x 10 x 0.25 cm
Seed beads, crystals, chicken
foot leather, synthetic suede,
snaps; peyote stitch, netting,
square stitch, bead embroidery
Photo by artist

B *Slaying Dragons 2*, 2011
Necklace: 43 x 1 cm;
Centerpiece: 8 x 5 cm
Seed beads, crystal pearls,
cubic zirconia briolette, curb
chain; herringbone stitch,
square stitch, right angle
weave, netting
Photo by artist

C *Fairy Ladder*, 2011
32 x 11 x 3.5 cm
Seed beads, cylinder beads,
crystal pearls; right angle
weave, peyote stitch
Photo by artist

C

GIVEN THAT YOU USED TO DO METALWORK, DO YOU INCORPORATE THAT INTO YOUR BEADWORK?
What a great question! The more I think about it, the more I realize how much of an influence my metalwork has had on my beaded jewelry. I tend to use a lot of metallic beads, and many of my designs reflect those that are more traditionally worked in metal, though the influences are more subtle now than they were a few years ago.

I've also done a lot of work with textiles. You can notice the influence of quilting in my use of shapes and layering, embroidery in the little details I like to add, and lacemaking in the techniques I use for my beading.

GIVE US A FEW ADJECTIVES TO BRIEFLY TELL US ABOUT YOUR STYLE.
My work is very feminine, but also has clean lines and a strong underlying structure. Years ago a friend called me a "bead engineer," and I like that description of myself. I studied architecture for a while, and I think that if I wasn't a jewelry designer, I might like to design bridges.

HOW DO YOU CHOOSE THE BEADS YOU USE?

I go through my beads and pull out colors that I like to see together, trying different combinations of hues and shades before I settle on a palette. When I buy beads, it's the "ooooh!" test—if I look at something and say, "oooh!," I buy it. I don't worry about what I will use it for; I know I will eventually find a way.

WHAT IMPACT HAS THE INTERNET HAD ON YOUR WORK?

Oh, wow—the Internet has changed everything. I was a beady hermit for the longest time. Most of the people I knew did not bead. And then the Internet happened. Suddenly, I was surrounded by literally hundreds of beaders all doing different things. I love looking at all the different styles and types of work, but even more than that, I love the online friendships. We share our work and our lives. I have Internet friends from around the globe who are now like sisters to me. We share our joys and sorrows, and I would trust them with my life. We like each others' work and we want to know the person who created it.

A

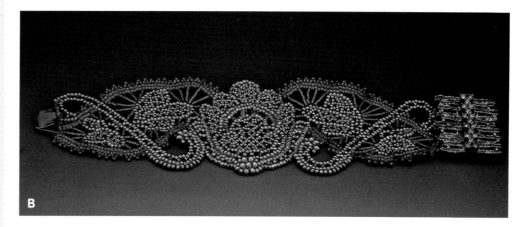

B

A *Celtic Knot*, 2011
Necklace: 43 x 2.5 cm;
Centerpiece: 11x 3 cm
Turquoise cabochon, seed beads, turquoise beads; right angle weave, cubic right angle weave, netting
Photo by artist

B *French Lace, 2011*
20 x 5.5 x 0.25 cm
Seed beads, cylinder beads, metal seed beads, purchased clasp; right angle weave, netting, square stitch
Photo by artist

HOW DOES YOUR ENVIRONMENT SHAPE YOUR WORK?

I'm very much inspired by the beauty of nature. I'm lucky to be living in close proximity to the ocean, the desert, and the hills. Living in wine country means that vineyards are also an inspiration; they're the perfect mix of nature and man-made scenery. The engineer in me loves the straight rows, while the artist in me loves the riotous colors, the lushness of the fruit, and the vines that do their best to escape their constraints.

TRACE FOR US HOW A TYPICAL DESIGN EVOLVES ONCE YOU FIND INSPIRATION.

That's tough to put into words: the real answer is, "I don't know." My inspirations are usually pretty nebulous; a sense of color, a shape, or just a feeling might set me off. I'll start pulling out beads and just play with them, trying a few stitches to see what happens. Usually I'll find some colors that set each other off, or a combination of stitches that creates a shape I like, and I'm off to the races.

C *My Soul Plays*, 2012
15 x 23 x 1 cm
Seed beads, metal seed beads, crystals, lampworked beads by Melissa Vess; embellished cubic right angle weave, embellished right angle weave
Photo by artist

D *Tribangle*, 2011
12 cm each side x 1 cm
Seed beads; right angle weave, netting, fringing
Photo by artist

DO YOU DRAW IDEAS FROM OTHER FORMS OF ARTISTIC EXPRESSION?

I love sculpture and paintings that emphasize line. I like art that flows; anything organic, but with an underlying structure. Art Nouveau is one of my favorite styles; it's sensual with a lot of motion, but it is also structured and stylized.

WHICH BEAD TECHNIQUES WOULD YOU LIKE TO EXPLORE IN FUTURE WORK?

I want to continue making lace with my beads, and I also want to do more dimensional work. I've been playing around with some unusual-shaped beads. I don't know where that will go yet, but I expect I have a lot more to do before I'm finished with them.

IF I DROPPED IN TO SEE YOUR BEAD STASH, WHAT WOULD I FIND?

Seed beads, for starters; I love those little points of color. I'm drawn to metallics, and I like to use a combination of neutrals and strong colors. Lampworked beads are another love of mine; my collection is out of control! I'm an unabashed lampworked bead hoarder. And crystals, of course—what would life be like without sparkle? I'm also

A

B

A *Time Travels,* 2012
Necklace: 43 x 4 cm;
Centerpiece: 14.5 x 8 cm
Soutache, seed beads, metal seed beads, crystal pearls, crystals, vintage buttons, onyx briolettes, pressed-glass beads, aluminum roses, watch parts, brass wire, synthetic suede, glue; bead embroidery, soutache embroidery, right angle weave, peyote stitch, netting
Photo by artist

B *Dance 'til Dawn,* 2011
20 x 4 x 1 cm
Seed beads, cylinder beads, metal seed beads, crystal pearls, crystals, vintage German rhinestones, synthetic suede, glue, clasp; bead embroidery, netting, peyote stitch, square stitch, herringbone stitch, fringing
Photo by artist

very fond of stones. I love their patterns and earthy colors. I think my stash has a little bit of everything in it; I'm a magpie. Good thing beads are small.

WHAT FEELINGS DO YOU WANT PEOPLE TO HAVE WHEN THEY SEE ONE OF YOUR PIECES?
I want them to smile. I want them to run their hands over the beads and smile some more. I think that beads are a very sensual medium, and I want the people who see my beadwork to feel that.

"There is a lightness and openness to Cynthia's pieces, giving them a lacy quality that is very appealing."

—MARCIA DECOSTER

C *Mariposa Reina*, 2012
19.5 x 4 x 0.25 cm
Seed beads, metal seed beads, crystals, clasp; right angle weave, herringbone stitch
Photo by artist

D *Mata Hari*, 2012
Necklace: 46 x 1 cm;
Centerpiece: 9 x 5.5 cm
Seed beads, vintage steel-cut beads, vintage points, cabochon by Sandy Spivey, vinyl tubing, synthetic suede, glue; bead embroidery, right angle weave, peyote stitch, netting
Photo by artist

D

A

I discovered the world of beads in 2004, and I was hooked. I mastered several beading techniques and started to design unique beaded jewelry. Six months later, I started a bead store, Hut Hashani, with my husband. Today we own two stores and I teach jewelry design to hundreds of students in Israel and sell the instructions over the Internet. I have published designs and tutorials in *Bead & Button* magazine, and hope to author a book of my own soon. I plan to never stop beading.

isabellalam.com

etsy.com/shop/bead4me

isabella lam

B

A *Fiore Pendant*, 2012
6 x 6 x 1 cm
Glass leaf beads, glass petal beads, round crystals, bicones, round seed beads, drop beads, wax cord, magnetic clasp, poly-ethylene thread; netting
Photo by artist

B *Cattleya Necklace*, 2012
44 x 3 x 0.3 cm
Superduo beads, crystal rose montees, bicones, round seed beads, drop beads, push box clasp, polyethylene thread; semi-herringbone stitch
Photo by artist

C *Arabesque Bouquet*, 2012
44 x 2.5 x 1 cm
Glass leaf beads, glass petal beads, fire-polished beads, rivolis, bicones, crystal drop beads, round seed beads, magnetic clasp, polyethylene thread; netting
Photo by artist

c

"Most of my pieces are born spontaneously; the beads together with my imagination lead me to each design. I start to bead according to a picture I see in my mind, then combine and match beads until I get what I desire."

HOW LONG HAVE YOU BEEN WORKING WITH BEADS?
I really became a creative beader after I started my bead store nearly a decade ago. Since then I have designed unique bead-works as well as many original jewelry tutorials that I have taught in my classes. In addition, I fashion tutorial instructions for making jewelry that is available through my web and Etsy sites.

I LOVE WHAT YOU'VE DONE BY INCLUDING THE SUPERDUOS IN YOUR WORK. HOW DO YOU OVERCOME THE CHALLENGES WHEN USING AN ENTIRELY NEW BEAD?
Unusual beads and shapes challenge me to craft new stories. Each piece of jewelry I make is unique. Some use new techniques

that I have developed, like the "Duo Kate" and "Duo Lace" pieces, while others combine familiar techniques in interesting ways. I start by seeing a picture of a jewel in my imagination, then combine and match beads until I am satisfied. I will never exhaust my yearning to create beaded jewelry that is inspired by the beauty in this world.

DOES THE INTERNET HAVE AN EFFECT ON YOUR ART?

The Internet is my window to the world of creativity, fashion, trends, and even color. I read about such things online and they influence my work. I also compare what I do with the work of other beading designers, trying to determine whether or not my jewelry is interesting and original, or whether I need to try harder to find a special touch.

WHO HAS GIVEN YOU ADVICE OVER THE INTERNET?

I have made a number of connections with other designers. For instance, Sabine Lippert's creations have intrigued and inspired me. I used her advice about using superduo beads, which soon became my favorites. I am looking forward to meeting her

A

B

C

D

A *Duo Kate Necklace*, 2012 (example #1, inspired by Kate Middleton)
45 x 6 x 0.3 cm
Superduo beads, bicones, round seed beads, drop beads, hook clasp, polyethylene thread; original technique, flat right angle weave, semi-herringbone stitch
Photo by artist

B *Duo Lace Bracelet*, 2012
17 x 3 x 0.5 cm
Superduo beads, crystals, bicones, cylinder beads, round seed beads, bugle beads, polyethylene thread; semi-herringbone stitch
Photo by artist

C & D *Duo Kate Necklace*, 2012 (example #2)
45 x 6 x 0.3 cm
Superduo beads, bicones, round seed beads, drop beads, hook clasp, polyethylene thread; original technique, flat right angle weave, semi-herringbone stitch
Photos by artist

in person one of these days. In addition, I have made contact with Ella Dess, whose tutorials and patterns are popular in Israel.

WHAT IS THE SPARK THAT IGNITES YOUR CREATIVITY?
Aside from the beads themselves, inspiration comes from the wonderful beauty of nature, which is the perfect creation. I find the changing of seasons to be amazing, phenomenal events. I may want to create a piece that reflects the peace of a winter snowfall, the colors of the ocean, or the flowering of cherry blossoms in the spring.

DO YOU HAVE A "BEADING PHILOSOPHY?"
Creating beaded jewelry is both fun and enjoyable. I hope that people will love the look of my jewelry as they wear these pieces, and that it helps them feel glamorous. Jewelry is simply a part of a total look and impression. The jewelry is not the main thing, the one who wears it is!

HOW MUCH PLANNING DO YOU DO BEFORE STARTING NEW PIECES?
Most of my pieces are born spontaneously as the beads in conjunction with my imagination lead me to each design. I have a picture in my mind, and I try different

A *Duo Kate Necklace,*
2012 (example #3)
45 x 6 x 0.3 cm
Superduo beads, bicones,
round seed beads, drop
beads, hook clasp,
polyethylene thread;
original technique,
flat right angle weave,
semi-herringbone stitch
Photo by artist

B *Duo Lace Bracelet,* 2012
17 x 3 x 0.5 cm
Superduo beads, crystals,
bicones, cylinder beads, round
seed beads, bugle beads,
polyethylene thread; semi-
herringbone stitch
Photo by artist

C

D

combinations of beads until I match that mental image. Sometimes it works perfectly, and other times I end up far from my imagined work.

DO YOU GRAVITATE TOWARD ANY PARTICULAR MATERIALS?

I have always found myself using a lot of crystals and Japanese seed beads, while I am delighted to have recently begun using superduo beads. I am fascinated by the endless options of this small, two-holed bead.

DO YOU HAVE ANY SECRETS TO SHARE ABOUT HOW TO SELECT BEADS FOR A PROJECT?

I don't plan the technique or the beads I will use, I just go with my inspiration and let the beads connect through me. My aim is to enhance the beauty and perfection of the woman who wears my jewelry.

C *Duo Lace Bracelet*, 2012
17 x 3 x 0.5 cm
Superduo beads, crystals, bicones, cylinder beads, round seed beads, bugle beads, polyethylene thread; semi-herringbone stitch
Photo by artist

D *Leya*, 2012
45 x 4.5 x 0.3 cm
Superduo beads, crystals, bicones, round seed beads, drop beads, polyethylene thread; right angle weave, semi-herringbone stitch
Photo by artist

"Texture is one of the first things to notice about Isabella's pieces. It makes you want to touch them!"

—MARCIA DECOSTER

Beading and all kinds of crafts have been my hobby since I was a little girl. I've been teaching beading classes for more than ten years, and I opened my own bead store, Das Perlament, in Bonn, Germany, in 2006. I love creating jewelry—it's so much fun. The precious friendships and wonderful connections are what make beading special for me. In addition, I am now an ambassador for Create Your Style with Swarovski Elements, and have published two bead books: *Das Perlenfest der Roses Montées* and *Perlen und Freundschaft.*

das-perlament.de

A

petra tismer

B

C

"Sparkling crystals of the finest quality give every piece of jewelry a special glow and feeling of luxury. In my work, I often combine crystals with seed beads and semiprecious stones."

A *Golden Sun*, 2010
5.5 x 1.3 cm
Crystals, seed beads; peyote stitch, netting
Photo by Christian Daitche

B *Just for Fun*, 2011
110 cm each
Crystals, wooden curtain rings wrapped with ribbons, various rings; stringing
Photo by Christian Daitche

C *Traveling to Milwaukee*, 2010
Short necklace: 45 cm;
Long necklace: 90 cm
Crystals, metal rings; stringing, right angle weave
Photo by Christian Daitche

COLOR IS EVERYWHERE IN YOUR WORK. HOW DO YOU DEVELOP YOUR VIBRANT PALETTES?
Color is a very important subject, and sometimes it takes me quite a while to make my decisions. For most jewelry, I prefer subtle colors because that makes my jewelry easy to combine with clothing. But I also love bright and colorful bead-work to brighten up gray, rainy days.

WHAT IS YOUR PERSONAL HISTORY WITH BEADING?
I have always been fas-cinated by beads, even when I was a schoolgirl, and they have accompa-nied me my whole life. As it turns out, all my needlework and other craft supplies have been sitting in boxes for the past ten years because my whole heart and at-tention now belong to my beads.

IS JEWELRY THE ONLY GENRE YOU WORK IN?
My main focus is to cre-ate jewelry that can be worn every day. Every once in a while I make key rings, bookmarks, or charms, which always make nice little gifts.

IN ADDITION TO BEADS, DO YOU ENGAGE IN OTHER ART OR CRAFT ACTIVITIES?
Needlework has been my hobby for many years, while cross-stitch and Hardanger

have fascinated me most. Believe it or not, working patiently for hours and hours with tiny stitches or with very small beads is heaven for me.

DO YOU LIKE TO PUSH THE ENVELOPE AND EXPERIMENT WITH YOUR WORK?

I love experiments and do not have a favorite technique. I like to come up with ideas for projects that will work as good examples for classes, to show others how much fun beading can be.

WHAT IS THE PROCESS LIKE FOR MAKING YOUR PIECES?

Often a collection of clothing leads me to create a harmoniously matching set of jewelry. First I figure out if a short or long necklace would look best, decide if I will need matching earrings or a bracelet. Once I have a basic plan, I try to find the perfect beads to make my new set of jewelry look just as I envisioned in my mind.

WHAT DO YOU CONSIDER WHEN SELECTING THE PERFECT SET OF BEADS FOR A PROJECT?

I think about the beads that will support my basic idea for a new set of jewelry. Bright colors and large beads are the perfect mixture

A

B

A *Curacao*, 2011
Necklace: 45 cm;
Bracelet: 19 cm
Crystals, fire-polished beads, seed beads; right angle weave
Photo by Christian Daitche

B *Rose*, 2010
20 cm
Rose quartz cabochons, seed beads; bead embroidery
Photo by Christian Daitche

C *Deep Blue Sea*, 2011
80 cm
Hand-painted ceramic beads, various large beads, seed beads, crystals; freestyle
Photo by Christian Daitche

D *Marmara*, 2012
Necklace: 45 cm;
Bracelet: 19 cm
Crystals, fire-polished beads, seed beads; right angle weave
Photo by Christian Daitche

C

D

to create a fun summer necklace; subtle and matte finishes will make elegant jewelry for everyday use. And then, for parties or a romantic candlelight dinner, shiny crystals and metallic beads are the perfect ingredients.

DO YOU USE THE INTERNET AS A TOOL FOR YOUR BEADING?
The Internet is a wonderful medium to keep in touch with my many beading friends from around the world. It is fascinating to see all of their beautiful creations and admire their work. I must admit I started using the Internet rather later than most people. But now I'm online often to inform my customers about classes and workshops.

WHAT TECHNIQUES ARE MOST PERTINENT RIGHT NOW?
My curiosity and my wish to assist customers have made me try many different beading techniques. Currently, I am fascinated with soutache and I am looking forward to playing with it more.

"Petra's beadwork crosses an array of styles, from organic and colorful to structured. She also shows us the use of repetitive elements to create classic jewelry."

—MARCIA DECOSTER

A

Personal adornment and expression of character and ideas through clothing has been a lifelong interest of mine. I have been creating wearable art for more than 40 years, in the form of theatrical costumes for the stage, competition clothing for ballroom dancers, and since 2007, beaded jewelry and accessories. In my beadwork, I find a deeply personal means of expression, inspired by the elegant beauty of the world around me.

www.hauteicebeadworks.blogspot.com

www.made4movement.com

marsha wiest-hines

B

A *Marigold Glade,* 2008
Focal: 7 x 8 x 1 cm;
Neck strap: 48 cm
Seed beads, cylinder beads, synthetic suede, labradorite cabochon, leaf beads, crystal bicones, nylon thread, adhesive; layered peyote stitch, fringing, Russian spiral weave
Photo by artist

B *Emerald Isle,* 2012
36 x 4 x 1 cm
Triangle, square, and rectangle crystal faceted jewels, seed beads, cylinder beads, nylon thread, vermeil box clasp, thread protectors; peyote stitch, triangle weave, layered netting
Photo by artist

C *Missing,* 2012
19 x 11 x 1 cm
Cylinder beads, seed beads, rivolis, bicones, clasp; peyote stitch, fringing
Photo by artist

C

"Beadwork is my hobby—my passionate, must-do-it pursuit. It is my art."

ASIDE FROM BEADS, WHAT OTHER MEDIA DO YOU ENJOY?

My "day job" is designing costumes, but I try to keep my beadwork separate from that. Using fabric would be logical, but my desire for separation keeps my beadwork fiber-free, except for many different kinds of thread. I don't like messy or wet media, either. Lampworking has a certain appeal, but the glass looks disturbingly liquid when hot. I like media that maintain their forms and don't make my fingers icky while I work.

OKAY, THAT LEADS ME TO ASK WHETHER YOUR CAREER AS A COSTUME DESIGNER INFLUENCES THE WAY YOU CREATE BEADWORK.

Oh, this is a million dollar question and I could answer it 50 different ways! I have learned an endless list of important things from making one-of-a-kind costumes. First and foremost, no one-off article is ever perfect, but if you do not aim for perfection at every step of the creation process, your results are doomed. Like custom dressmaking, my beading follows a "two-steps-forward-one-step-back process." And I have learned there is nothing new under the sun.

TELL US HOW YOU GOT INTERESTED IN BEADING AND JEWELRY.

I was given two gifts on my birthday in 2007 that started my journey with beads. One was a strung bracelet with a difficult clasp that was much too big for me. I looked at it and thought, "How hard could it be to make this smaller and replace the clasp?" I also received a gift certificate to Barnes and Noble, where I saw Lark's *500 Beaded Objects* on the bookshelf. I opened that book and was instantly hooked—I wanted to do that!

WHAT SPARKS YOUR CREATIVE FLAME?

I create based on the beauty outdoors. I want to share the natural glory I see. I love holding a needle and thread and manipulating it. I love designing in three dimensions with consideration for wearing and movement. I love sparklies and color. And I love that a human body can be a gallery for displaying art.

WHERE ELSE DO YOU LOOK FOR INSPIRATION?

I am fond of the photography found in Google Images because it answers questions: What does wisteria look like? How is the structure of a lilac leaf different from a maple leaf? What are the phases of the moon? And literature provides a catalyst for me as well, because the joy of analysis and interpretation of character is firmly lodged in costume designers' souls.

A

B

C

A *Ash & Ember—the Balrog*, 2011
40 cm x 11 x 1.5 cm
Seed beads, cylinder beads, crystal faceted jewels, fire-polished beads, polyethylene thread, nylon thread, blackened clasp; peyote stitch, netting, stringing
Photos by artist

B & C *Vera Similitude Walks the Red Carpet*, 2009
Focal: 12 x 10 x 1 cm;
Strap: 15 cm
Seed beads, cylinder beads, faceted crystals and bicones, metal rose beads, polyethylene thread; peyote stitch
Photos by artist

CAN YOU OUTLINE YOUR DESIGN PROCESS FOR US?
Sometimes I draw and plan, and sometimes I collect materials and just figure it out as I go. It's important to listen to the materials and not make them do things they do not want to. I feel free to rework pieces several times, until a good solution to a problem appears.

WHAT ONLINE RELATIONSHIPS HAVE YOU DEVELOPED AND HOW HAVE THEY INFLUENCED YOU?
Well, I have become involved in the "Battle of the Beadsmith." Additionally, I consider myself friends with the inimitable Steven Weiss, and with such wonderful beaders as Sue Horine, Nancy Dale (see page 52), Linda Roberts, Cynthia Newcomer Daniel (see page 80), Sigi Contreras, Patrick Duggan (see page 16), Eva Maria Keiser, Zoya Gutina (see page 142), Hannah Rosner, Kinga Nichols (see page 120) ... gosh, I could list a hundred other folks! The energy of artists presenting work worldwide is palpable and contagious, and provides support as well as information about techniques and resources.

A

B

A *Poseidon's Garden*, 2012
37 x 12 x 1 cm
Seed beads, cylinder beads,
rivolis, navette jewels, pearls,
polyethylene thread; peyote
stitch, fringing, netting
Photo by artist

B *Forget Me Knot
Bracelet*, 2012
17 x 2.5 x 0.5 cm
Seed beads, crystal bicones,
polyethylene thread;
triangle weave
Photo by artist

C *Calypso's Valentine*, 2010
Focal: 8 x 8 x 1.5 cm;
Neck strap: 54 cm
Seed beads, split fossilized
ammonite, freshwater pearls,
nylon thread, brass toggle
clasp, shell buttons;
peyote stitch, netting,
fringing, stringing
From the private collection
of Cathy Dessert with her kind
permission
Photo by artist

C

WHAT DO YOU STILL WANT TO LEARN ABOUT BEADING?

I am determined to learn bead crochet, but that seems an elusive technique. I have read about it, and even seen video tutorials, but I suspect this will require a real-life teacher.

WHAT DO YOU LIKE TO CREATE IN ADDITION TO JEWELRY?

I love the way beadwork frames and embellishes the face, so I've made a couple of hats. I may someday try a beaded bag, or shoe, or belt.

WHAT FEELINGS DO YOU WANT YOUR BEADED WORK TO STIR IN VIEWERS?

Every piece should be timeless, not trendy, and suggest its inspiration. Pieces have a mood or character I want to convey. For example, "Ash & Ember—the Balrog," is about the demonic, titan-like beings from *Lord of the Rings*. I wanted it to evoke menace, danger, and embers ready to burst into flame. But I also wanted it to be a beautiful, wearable piece of jewelry.

"Marsha's pieces share a huge sparkle factor as she brings seed beads and crystals together, showcasing the large, fancy stones in beautifully arranged design."

—MARCIA DECOSTER

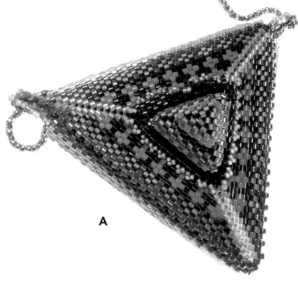

A

I am a published author, designer, and international teacher known for dimensional beadwork designs. I began beading at the age of ten and have now enjoyed more than 40 years of bead exploration. In addition to precise, technically innovative work, I enjoy teaching and sharing my designs with students around the world, performing as a bead ambassador to spread the joy, benefits, and creative fulfillment of beadwork and to ensure it will continue evolving in the future.

spiritbead.net

christina vandervlist

"The smaller the bead, the more I love it! I love great detail and interesting structure, and the various sizes and shapes, finishes and colors, all have their uses."

B

C

A & B *Triptych Pocket*, 2012
7 x 8 x 1 cm
Glass cylinder beads, glass seed
beads, round beads, beading
thread; dimensional even-count
peyote stitch
Photos by artist

B *Coral Lariat*, 2012
80 x 5 x 2 cm
Glass seed beads, fire-polished
faceted glass beads, beading
thread; tubular, single, spiral, and
inclusion herringbone stitches
Photo by artist

WHERE DOES YOUR PERSONAL STORY WITH BEADS BEGIN?

I have 40 years of bead-ing experience; I began at age ten (in self-defense, a great story) and have always beaded in some capacity, from costume embellishment in my years as a performing artist, to self-expression as a working mother.

WOW, 40 YEARS! HOW WOULD YOU SAY YOUR WORK HAS EVOLVED OVER THIS SPAN?

My work is becoming more and more technically innovative and encompasses greater precision in structural integrity and engineered design than before. At the same time, certain elements are becoming more fluid. I've begun integrating these two opposing concepts in my current work and find they create a dynamic tension that is very exciting.

HAVE YOUR LIFE'S EXPE-RIENCES INFORMED YOUR BEADING DESIGNS?

My background is in act-ing, singing, and dancing. I was also taught how to teach. This background, as well as my work as a Certified Zentangle Teacher (CZT), has honed both my teaching and my observational skills, which are essential tools in my ability to create and educate.

DESCRIBE THE DEVELOPMENT PROCESS FOR YOUR WONDERFULLY TEXTURED DESIGNS.

I like to play! I'll take appealing beads and see what happens with various combinations of stitch or color or proportion. I'll use "what if" moments and run with them, creating small samplers of ideas until one refuses to let go of my imagination and demands to be brought into being.

WHAT INTRIGUES YOU ABOUT USING THE INTERNET WITH YOUR WORK?

The Internet is a great tool for enabling distant colleagues to exchange ideas and collaborate. It provides immediate access to resources, from material suppliers to inspirational sites such as museums and architectural collections. The Internet helps people who cannot otherwise meet to form friendships that provide support, encouragement, inspiration, and critical input, all of which are invaluable to any artist.

IN WHAT WAYS DO OTHER ARTISTIC MEDIA ENHANCE AND INSPIRE YOUR BEADING?

I particularly love any kind of needlework, as well as drawing, sketching, and painting. The change of pace can spark new explorations in beadwork. The random mingling of watercolors can inspire a new color palette, while stitching may generate an idea for new shapes and structures to be incorporated into my beadwork.

104

A

A *Tempting Tendrils,* 2012
36 x 9 x 2 cm
Glass seed beads, brass round bead, brass head pin, wire, metal floral elements; spiral peyote stitch, square stitch, wire wrapping
Photo by artist

B *Mrs. Poe's Sunday Necklace,* 2012
52 x 5 x 3 cm
Jump rings, prefabricated metal beads, elements, chain, wire, round stone beads (iron pyrite, onyx, smoky quartz, agate), glass seed beads; tubular herringbone stitch, modified right angle weave, wire wrapping
Photo by artist

C *Eye Candy,* 2012
8 x 8 x 2 cm
Plastic round beads, glass drop beads, glass lentil beads, beading thread; cubic right angle weave
Photo by artist

B

C

DO YOU SET OUT TRYING TO EVOKE ANY SPECIFIC TYPE OF REACTION FROM YOUR AUDIENCE?
I would like them to be inspired so that they try something new in their own work. My ideal is to offer inspiration to others, to provoke their thoughts so they ask, "How is this possible?" and "Can I really do this, too?" I hope people looking at my work will want to begin or further their own journey of discovery using beads as an expressive medium.

HOW DO YOU DECIDE WHICH BEADS TO USE FOR A PARTICULAR PROJECT?
I select my beads by the amount of detail I expect to achieve—which ones will best serve that purpose. I also consider the finish and color, because these have a strong impact on the appearance and structure of the final work. It's also important to understand what the wearer of a finished piece is likely to experience, as certain beads lend themselves to either everyday or special-occasion wear.

"From incredibly engineered to textured tendrils, Christina's pieces cover a broad range of styles."
—MARCIA DECOSTER

A

Linda L. Jones, who passed away in 2012, lived in Halifax, Nova Scotia, where she designed, created, and taught beadwork for 35 years. Her work has appeared in *Bead & Button* magazine, and in their annual book, *Creative Beading, Volume 4,* as well as in several exhibitions. She sold her beading pieces beginning in 1985 through fine craft galleries in Ontario, Nova Scotia, and Quebec. She often worked free-form and noted, "I frequently bead myself into corners."

linda l. jones

"I love the meditative aspect of simply doing the beadwork and mastering new stitches. I think of beadwork as a form of meditation."

B

A *Lush—Lace Earrings,* 2011
3.8 x 2.5 cm
Rayon lace, seed beads, flat-back crystals, brass beads, metal findings; hand painting, embellishment
Photo by artist

B *Spring Conjunction,* 2010
16.5 x 7.6 cm
Seed beads, dichroic cabochons, fire-polished beads, lampworked glass bead, synthetic suede, sterling silver slide clasp; bead embroidery
Photo by artist

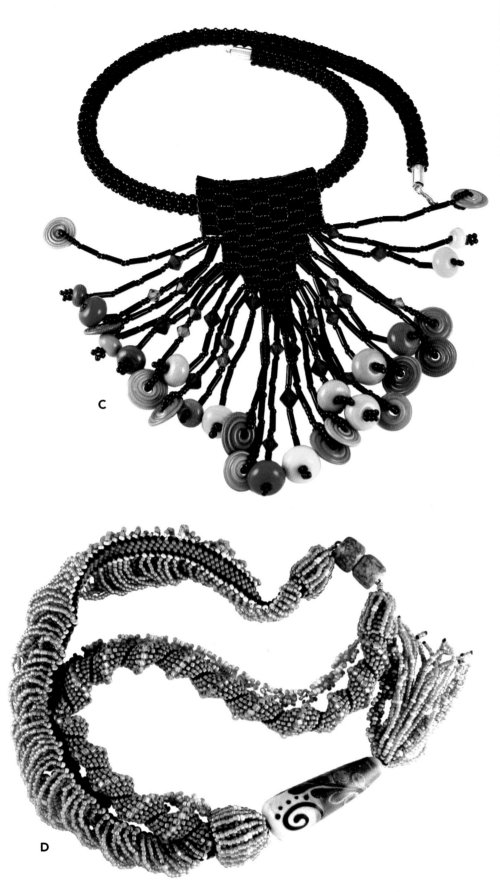

C *Merry Goth*, 2009
Necklace: 47 cm;
Dangle: 2.4 cm
Seed beads, bugle beads, lampworked
glass disks, braided leather rope, ster-
ling silver hook-and-eye clasp; square
stitch, right angle weave
Photo by artist

D *Serendipity*, 2010
55.9 cm
Lampworked focal bead, polymer clay
over metal screw-clasp, seed beads;
Cellini spiral stitch, Dutch spiral stitch,
spiral stitch, square stitch
Photo by artist

**LET'S GO BACK IN
TIME. WHEN AND HOW
DID YOU BEGIN WITH
BEADS?**

I always loved the look
of beadwork. In my 20s
I bought a little hobby
loom and followed
written instructions to
make bracelets. Even-
tually, I met a Native
woman who taught me
how to do peyote stitch
and make earrings with
beads and quills. Next,
I became friends with
a man who taught me
right angle weave. I
kept beading as a hobby
for years. Eventually,
the craft began to boom
and my work evolved
into a business.

**WHO INTRODUCED YOU
TO BEADING?**

I've had a couple of
mentors, but I am
primarily self-taught,
in the sense that I have
learned from an excel-
lent selection of books.
Most classes are out
of reach from the east
coast of Canada, so I've
learned to follow (and
value) excellent written
and illustrated instruc-
tion. Where there's a
will … there's a book!

**WHICH ONLINE
RESOURCES IN THE
BEAD COMMUNITY DO
YOU USE MOST OFTEN?**

I check Facebook daily,
as it is the handiest way
to see the latest work
of beaders from all over
the world. I read sev-
eral blogs, and check

for Favorites on Flickr. For me, Facebook seems to be the most up-to-date and comprehensive way to view new work.

I originally signed up for Facebook to market my work, but it turned out to be far more than a marketing tool. I made connections with many bead artists from all over the world, forming friendships that have been valuable sources of practical advice, support, and inspiration.

HOW ABOUT RELATING A FAVORITE "ONLINE" STORY?
Nancy Dale (see page 52) asked to be added as a friend on Facebook a while ago. At that time, she was happily obsessed with learning beadwork—but not designing. But before long she worked up the nerve to start making her own patterns, and then took off like a rocket. She has become, in my humble opinion, one of the best designers in the world. It was a complete joy to watch her evolve and become such a star.

DO YOU HAVE A BLOG?
I blogged under Wild Wicked Beads for some time and love writing, but health problems made me suspend operations. I loved the interchange on the blog—the direct feedback; plus I got to know some interesting people. It was a great place to talk about the challenges of the craft.

A

A *Caribbean—Lace Earrings*, 2011
11.4 x 3.8 cm
Rayon lace, seed beads, flat-back crystal, crystals, metal findings; hand painting, embellishment
Photo by artist

B *Gauntlet for a Saturn Return*, 2008
Embroidery: 12.7 x 17.8 cm;
Netting: 11.4 x 17.8 cm
Seed beads, fire-polished beads, honey calcite stone, garnet beads, bead backing material, synthetic suede, hook-and-eye closure; backstitch embroidery, peyote stitch, netting
Photo by Alex Chisholm

C *Watergarden*, 2010
50.8 cm
Graveyard plume agate, seed beads, 24-karat gold-plated clasp, synthetic suede; peyote stitch
Photo by artist

B

C

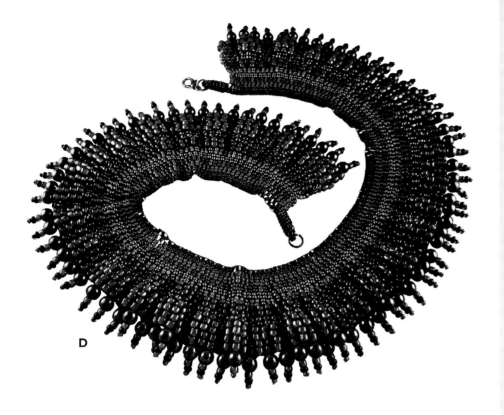

WHAT ABOUT METHOD—WHAT CAN YOU TELL US ABOUT THE WAY YOU WORK?
My work is all about color—and flying by the seat of my pants! But I obsess about color, and what is actually wearable.

WHERE DO YOUR IDEAS AND INSPIRATION COME FROM?
From textiles of all kinds, colors in the landscape, paintings, other bead artists, . . . really everything and anything.

HOW HAS YOUR WORKING PROCESS EVOLVED OVER TIME?
As someone who prefers to work free-form whenever possible, I've learned to do more thinking at the front end.

WHAT'S YOU FAVORITE PART OF WORKING WITH BEADS?
Again, color. And light. And getting to the point, in a new piece, where I stop wondering whether I've spent 25 hours making a disaster.

WHAT RESPONSES DO YOU GET TO YOUR WORK?
Generally responses are very enthusiastic. I'm quite astonished by it sometimes because I'm more familiar than many people with what fabulous works are out there.

D *Rust Collar,* 2009
55.9 x 7.6 cm
Seed beads, glass beads, copper findings; peyote stitch
Photo by artist

E & F *I'm Just Wild about Saffron,* 2010
16.5 x 5 cm
Brass form, seed beads, glass button focal, pearls, crystal pearls, Bali silver beads, synthetic suede; bead embroidery, peyote stitch
Photos by artist

"Linda's work exhibits a masterful use of vibrant color and shows her willingness to explore unexpected media."

—MARCIA DECOSTER

A

gabriella van diepen

Born in the Netherlands to a Caribbean father and a Dutch mother, I have always been aware of other cultures, other languages, other colors and flavors—always aware, but never connected. I explore this in my work, where I search for ways to express personal experiences. I've worked in many different media, initially as a hobby while pursuing a career as a biomedical scientist. I started beading a little more than five years ago after moving to the United States, and decided to follow my true passion as a full-time artist.

gabroen.blogspot.com

"I would like my jewelry to stimulate the senses and evoke desire. I want viewers to covet my jewelry for what it is, without thinking of whether it matches a particular piece of their wardrobe."

A *Have the Stomach to Party Purse*, 2011
19 x 12 x 6 cm
Mother-of-pearl cabochon, vintage cabochons, crystal pearls, tiger eye beads, bugle beads, vintage crystals, seed beads, purse leather, foundation, thread; peyote stitch, bead embroidery
Photo by Jeroen Medema

B *Baas*, 2012
63 x 25 x 16 cm
Rivolis, seed beads, vintage African trade beads, leather flowers, African wooden mask, adhesive, grout, thread; modified right angle weave, peyote stitch, two-drop peyote and tubular peyote stitches, netting, grouting
Photo by Jeroen Medema

B

ALL OF YOUR PIECES HAVE A SURPRISE TUCKED SOMEWHERE WITHIN THEM, WHETHER IT IS A FORM, A COLOR, OR A STORY. DO YOU PLAN THIS FROM THE BEGINNING, OR DOES IT EVOLVE AS PART OF THE PROCESS?
My pieces always evolve. I start with a plan based on a focal element and color. The plan always changes and sometimes turns into a story. I also like to add a deliberate imperfection, in most cases a random red bead, as a symbol of gratitude for my creative gift.

HOW LONG HAVE YOU BEEN WORKING WITH BEADS AS THE MEDIUM FOR YOUR ART?
I strung my first necklace five years ago.

WHICH OTHER MEDIA HAVE YOU WORKED WITH?
I've used fabric, leather, embroidery thread, paint, and dyes. Free embroidery has taught me to persist. The creativity is always there, but channeling it into a coherent result never comes easy. Lately, I'm combining these media with my beadwork, such as the piece I call "Baas."

HOW WOULD YOU CHARACTERIZE YOUR WORK?
My work is becoming more and more storytelling, using symbolism and a strong sense of color.

WHERE DO YOU FIND INSPIRATION FOR YOUR WORK?
In a number of places, primarily in nature's colors, free embroidery, fabric art, and tribal art.

A *Minotaur*, 2012
29 x 18 x 1 cm
Kabamba jasper cabo-
chon, seed beads, vintage
drops, button, foundation,
adhesive, synthetic suede,
thread; peyote stitch,
bead embroidery
Photo by Jeroen Medema

B Untitled, 2012
12 x 2.5 x 1 cm
Crystal rhinestones, seed
beads, crystal bicones,
vintage drop beads,
foundation, adhesive,
synthetic suede, thread,
ear wires; peyote stitch,
bead embroidery
Photo by Jeroen Medema

C *Van Gogh's Blossom-
ing Acacia Branch*, 2010
5.4 x 14 x 0.5 cm
Seed beads, bugle
beads, vintage button,
foundation, adhesive,
synthetic suede, thread;
bead embroidery
Photo by Jeroen Medema

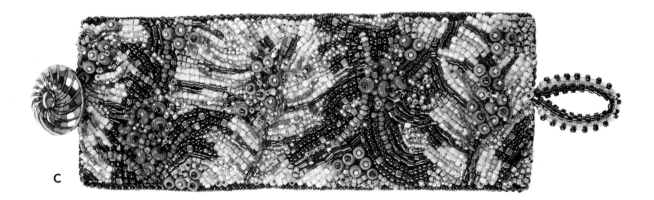

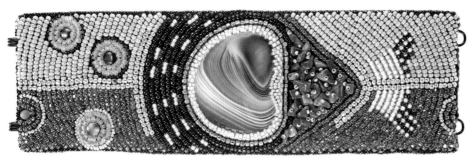

D

E

D *Cosmosis*, 2012
16 x 5 x 0.5 cm
Agate, seed beads, foundation, adhesive, synthetic suede,
thread, hook-and-eye closure;
peyote stitch, bead embroidery
Photo by Jeroen Medema

E Untitled, 2012
17 x 16 x 1 cm
Rivolis, obsidian, vintage metallic
faux pearls, pearls, seed beads,
leather foundation, adhesive,
synthetic suede, thread;
bead embroidery
Photo by Jeroen Medema

HOW DO YOUR DESIGNS DEVELOP AND COME TO FRUITION?
I start with something as a focal point, work out a color scheme around it, and then work persistently while being open to changes as the piece evolves.

HAS THE INTERNET MADE A DIFFERENCE IN YOUR BEADING?
An artistic mind is curious and not easily satisfied. The Internet feeds me almost lim-itlessly. It's a visual stimulus and a link to the world around me.

In addition, creating art is a mostly solitary act, but the online art community allows me to work together remotely and provide/receive feedback and encouragement.

WHICH BEAD TECH-NIQUES WOULD YOU LIKE TO EXPLORE IN FUTURE WORK?
I would like to ex-plore the possibilities of three-dimensional sculptural beadwork.

IS JEWELRY THE MAIN FOCUS OF YOUR ART, OR ARE THERE ADDITIONAL FORMS OF BEADWORK YOU ENJOY MAKING?
Jewelry was my main focus when I started, but I'm shifting my in-terest to nonwearables.

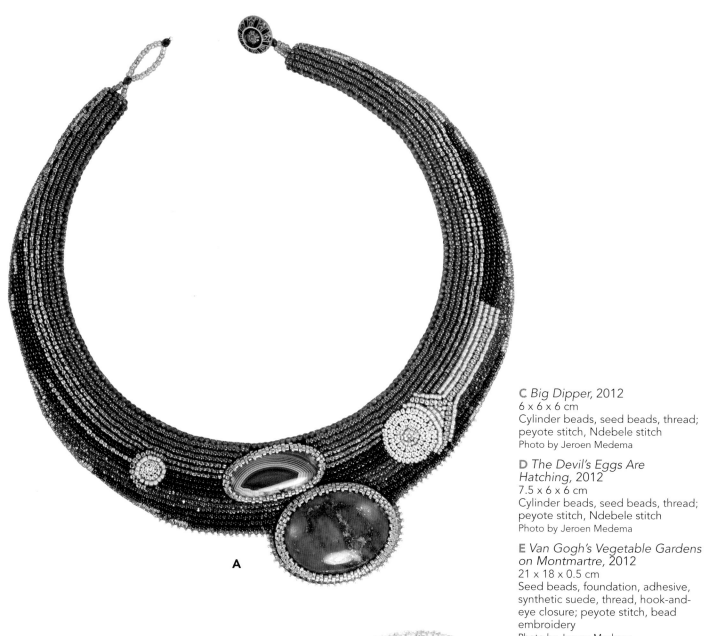

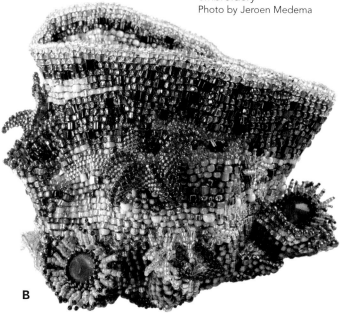

C *Big Dipper,* 2012
6 x 6 x 6 cm
Cylinder beads, seed beads, thread;
peyote stitch, Ndebele stitch
Photo by Jeroen Medema

D *The Devil's Eggs Are
Hatching,* 2012
7.5 x 6 x 6 cm
Cylinder beads, seed beads, thread;
peyote stitch, Ndebele stitch
Photo by Jeroen Medema

E *Van Gogh's Vegetable Gardens
on Montmartre,* 2012
21 x 18 x 0.5 cm
Seed beads, foundation, adhesive,
synthetic suede, thread, hook-and-
eye closure; peyote stitch, bead
embroidery
Photo by Jeroen Medema

A *Night Sky,* 2012
19 x 18 x 1 cm
Agate and lapis lazuli cabochons,
seed beads, vintage button,
foundation, adhesive, synthetic
suede, thread; peyote stitch,
bead embroidery
Photo by Jeroen Medema

B *Reef Bowl,* 2011
35 x 10 cm
Seed beads, bugle beads, rivolis,
thread; peyote stitch, brick stitch,
Ndebele stitch, branch fringe,
embellishment
Photo by Jeroen Medema

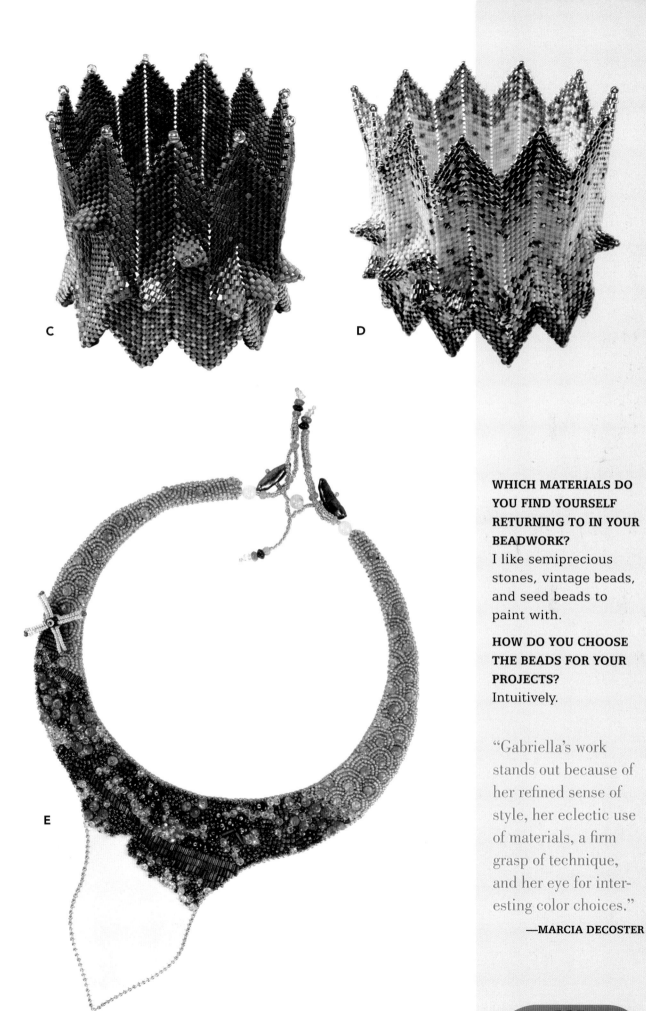

C

D

E

A

idele gilbert

My beadwork is a culmination of my interest in needlework techniques that I have loved all my life. Born in St. Paul, Minnesota, I moved to Southern California in 1967 when I married my husband, Harry. I have been active in the Embroiderers' Guild of America since 1972. My interests in creative arts have included making miniatures and all forms of needlework. I was introduced to beading in 1995 through the Guild. After learning beading techniques at a variety of bead classes, I began designing my own beaded creations and teaching beading locally.

idelegilbert.com

"I am interested in pushing the envelope. I like to sculpt with beads to make little boxes, miniature bears, and unusual beaded pieces that have never been done before. I like to add a bit of whimsy to my designs."

A *Mouse Thimble Holder and Pincushion,* 2009
6 x 3 x 5 cm
Seed beads, pearls, semiprecious stones, nylon thread, wool batting, synthetic suede, wire, sterling silver thimble embellished with cat designs; bead embroidery
Photo by Harry Gilbert

B *Miniature Beaded Bears,* 2007
3.5 x 2 x 1.5 cm
Seed beads, nylon thread, synthetic suede; peyote stitch. The bears are jointed five ways
Photo by Harry Gilbert

B

C

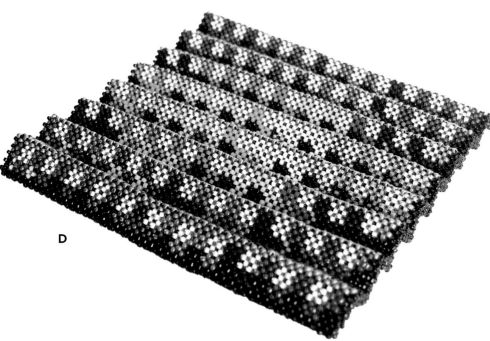

D

MANY OF YOUR BRILLIANT DESIGNS ARE IN MINIATURE WITH AMAZING DETAIL. WHY DO YOU BEAD IN MINIATURE, AND WHAT ARE THE CHALLENGES?
I have a fascination with making tiny things. With beading, I love using vintage micro miniature beads. My greatest difficulty is the beading needles. I use size 16, but they are still too big to go through some of the smallest micro beads.

HOW DO YOU GET STARTED WITH IDEAS FOR PROJECTS?
My interest in trompe l'oeil (fool the eye) has influenced my bead art. I like to see if I can recreate items using beads as my medium, such as my parakeets. I am also a collector of antique sewing items. My antique pieces have

C *Blue and Green Parakeet Boxes*, 2010
4.5 x 15 x 4 cm
Seed beads, nylon thread, wire, beads; peyote stitch. The parakeets have jointed heads and separately attached wings, are hollow, and open in the middle with a peyote-stitched sliding hinge
Photo by Harry Gilbert

D *Cubic Right Angle Weave Abstract Sculpture, View One*, 2012
15 x 14.5 x 1.5 cm
Seed beads, nylon thread; cubic right angle weave
Photo by Harry Gilbert

inspired me to make my beaded pincushions, beaded fish, and seahorse etui boxes.

IS IT SIZE, OR COLOR, OR WHAT THAT YOU LOOK FOR WHEN BUYING BEADS?

I am attracted to size 15° seed beads and smaller, but I also use size 11° seed beads or cylinder beads, depending on the project. I like to remind myself that I am actually sculpting with glass. I am dazzled by bead colors, but I am also concerned about buying good-quality beads that will not fade or have the color come off. The beads I use must fit the requirements of the project I am planning to make.

DO YOU MAKE OTHER MINIATURE CREATIONS IN ADDITION TO BEADS?

I have carved 1-inch (2.5 cm) miniature wooden peg dolls. I once created a miniature needlework shop with miniature painted canvases. I carved all the furniture and upholstered the tiny chairs with petit point. I have also painted special-order needlepoint canvases and designed pop-up patterns for rubber stamps. I have designed and stitched original-design molas (reverse appliqué).

DO YOU COMPLETELY PLAN YOUR BEAD SCULPTURES BEFORE STARTING WORK?

When I get an idea for a project, I mentally figure out how the whole structure will fit together. Then I make a sketch of the design. My completed projects usually look very much like my original drawing.

A

B

C

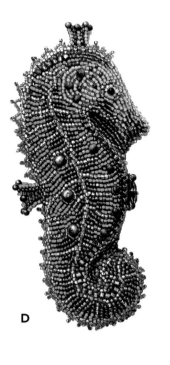

D

E

A *Micro Miniature Beaded Bears*, 2007
3 x 2 x 1.5 cm and 2 x 1 x 1 cm
Vintage seed beads, nylon thread,
synthetic suede; peyote stitch
Photo by Harry Gilbert

B & C *The Aquarium and The Green
House*, 2011
Aquarium: 3 x 5 x 4 cm;
Greenhouse: 3.5 x 5 x 3.5 cm
Seed beads, nylon thread; double-sided
right angle weave, cubic right angle weave
Photo by Harry Gilbert

D & E *Seahorse Etui Box and Fish Etui
Box*, 2009
Seahorse: 15 x 6 x 2.5 cm;
Fish: 4 x 12 x 3 cm
Seed beads, pearls, nylon thread, hand-
made wire hinges, synthetic suede; bead
embroidery
Photo by Harry Gilbert

**HAS THE INTERNET AFFECTED
HOW YOU DO BUSINESS?**
Yes, I present my bead
artistry and sell my patterns
to an international audience
through my website and
my blog. Sending the
patterns as PDF files makes
it easy for the buyer and
me to connect. I include
color charts with detailed
instructions, which help
bridge language differences.

Also, I've collected 40 years'
worth of magazine clippings
that give me ideas for projects
(I wish I could get organized
enough to actually find what
I am looking for in all those
little pieces of paper). But the
Internet has made it much
easier to search for images on
any subject.

**HOW DO YOU HOPE TO
AFFECT THOSE WHO SEE
YOUR WORK?**
I strived for the WOW factor
from people viewing my
beadwork, and I usually get
that reaction.

"Idele takes beading in
miniature to new heights
with her sense of playfulness and exquisite atten-
tion to detail."

—MARCIA DECOSTER

I was born in Europe, where I studied art throughout my school years, then came to the United States in my teens, when I first started painting murals. I later discovered and fell in love with bead embroidery, which I now use most usually in the form of cuff bracelets to tell stories and interpret fairy tales, myths, and the world around us. I currently live in Boulder, Colorado, with my husband, Paul, and canine muse, Samantha Regina, who sports a significant underbite.

crimsonfrogdesigns.
blogspot.com

A

kinga nichols

B

A *Presence #1 and Presence #2*, 2012
16 x 5.5 cm each
Brass cuffs, lambskin, various seed beads, art cabochons by Nix Creations, squirrel fur, pearls, tila beads; bead embroidery, peyote stitch
Photo by artist

B *Autumn Snail*, 2012
16 x 6 cm
Bronze focal by artist, various seed beads, crystals, pearls; bead embroidery
Photo by artist

C

> "Jewelry has a purpose beyond viewing. It is art, but you can fondle it, wear it, and enjoy it in other ways than you would enjoy a painting. You interact with it more. It's tactile, it warms to your touch, and becomes a temporary extension of you."

D

C *Octopus Bracelet*, 2012
17 x 6.5 cm
Various seed beads, pearls, crystals, taxidermy eye; bead embroidery
Photo by artist

D *Furry Eyeball Bracelet Trio*, 2012
16 x 4.5 cm
Aluminum cuff, lambskin, doll eyes, spike beads, seed beads; bead embroidery, peyote stitch
Photo by artist

YOUR BEAD-EMBROIDERED WORK IS BOTH FANCIFUL AND COLORFUL. WHAT INSPIRES THESE WHIMSICAL CREATIONS?
Memories, colors, and textures that are all around waiting for me to make them my playthings. Even a smell sometimes generates multiple ideas. Little do we realize that olfactory sensations affect our moods and feelings so profoundly. The smell of fallen leaves on a rainy autumn day can be the start of creating ten different things.

HOW DID YOU ARRIVE AT WORKING WITH BEADS?
I painted murals and have used oil and acrylic to paint on many surfaces, from glass to wood, even children's faces. With each different medium, the same stories and imaginings emerged. So to me, beading is just a logical but more introverted continuation of what I have always been doing. I still tell stories. It's just on a smaller, more intimate scale now.

WHERE DO YOU FIND YOUR DESIGN INSIGHTS?
Inspiration is within possibilities—where many see a concrete world set in stone, I see possibilities. If I find an element that evokes childhood memories, or reminds me of something I read,

I let my imagination run wild. Nature is inspiring, too. But in many ways I live in my imagination, so that's where things usually start for me.

I might add, designs ideas often keep me awake at night. I sketch these designs and bead them like they always existed and I just plucked them from a dream tree. It's almost like backward engineering, but of course the piece only exists in my head.

GIVE ME A SENTENCE THAT TELLS US ABOUT THE TYPE OF WORK YOU DO.

These are visual diaries of my life, where dogs can become heroes, eyeballs are watching me from the dark, and everything tells a tale.

IN WHAT OTHER ARTISTIC GENRES DO YOU FIND INSPIRATION?

I like to listen to music while beading. There are other influences as well. For example, Klimt's paintings are an eternal source of inspiration; and stories and literary works, from the Brothers Grimm through H. P. Lovecraft, and Tolkien to Kurt Vonnegut.

IS THE INTERNET A BIG PART OF YOUR BEADING LIFE?

It's huge! It allows me to connect to a "hive mind" of artists around the globe to discuss techniques and share inspiration. It's a great feeling to share my love of beads with people who are equally crazy about them. Online challenges and contests allow the beading community to learn, work, and grow together. Also, I am able to sell my work online.

A *Viking Buddha,* 2012
16 x 6 cm
Antique bronze Buddha focal, tila beads, crystals, various seeds beads; bead embroidery
Photo by artist

B *Four Seasons Collection of Spring, Summer, Fall, and Winter Cuffs,* 2011–2012
17 x 6 cm
Various seed beads, pearls, crystal with sheepskin backing; bead embroidery
Photo by artist

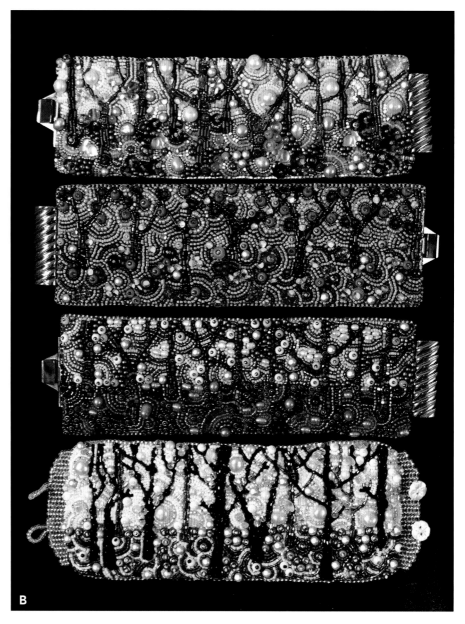

C

D

C *Octopus Neckpiece*, 2012
43 x 28 cm
Brass neck cuff, taxidermy eye,
various seed beads, pearls,
crystals, coral; bead embroidery
Photo by artist

D *My Mine*, 2011
16 x 6 cm
Crystals, heavy metal seed
beads; bead embroidery
Photo by artist

E *Sammy's Fishies*, 2012
43.2 x 33 cm
Seed beads, pearls, crystals,
clasp, taxidermy eyes, lambskin backing; bead embroidery
Photo by artist

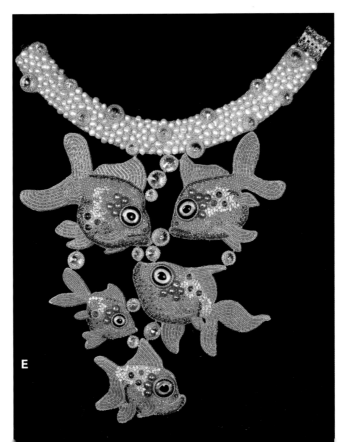

E

**SO, I TAKE IT YOU HAVE
A LOT OF ONLINE BEAD-
ING FRIENDS NOW.**
Yes. I've met so many
artists who have be-
come really good friends.
I would never have
known them if not for
the Internet, but I could
not imagine my life now
without them! When a
beader goes from not
knowing anyone who is as
passionate about the art to
having friends who get ex-
actly what they are talking
about, life gets easier and
inspiration never leaves
their side. That is the biggest influence the Internet
has on me.

**WHERE DO YOU SEE
YOURSELF HEADED IN
FUTURE WORK?**
I recently purchased a
kiln and want to ex-
periment with making
more of my own com-
ponents—stuff like PMC
and glass. So instead of
more bead techniques,
I would rather expand
my repertoire, where the
finished piece contains
more of my own work
in the form of focals,
clasps, and other compo-
nents made by me.

"Elaborately embel-
lished bead embroi-
dery with lots of color,
texture, and whimsy
is the signature of
Kinga's fun pieces."

—**MARCIA DECOSTER**

A

I was a kid who did my math homework only so I could use my prized colored markers to make awesome graphs. Later I went to art school for graphic design. I subsequently followed my California dream, where I worked as a display designer. With two other jewelry friends, I produced a private show for 13 years, which is when I began making jewelry in earnest. And I still love the art of beadweaving after all these years. My work has been published in Marcia DeCoster's *Beaded Opulence* and *500 Beaded Jewelry*, and was a Bead Dreams 2010 finalist in "Passion of the Pen."

susan blessinger

"I strive to keep my bead designs looking effortless, which is ironic because the very nature of beading can be the ultimate in precision and detail."

A *Picasso's Feathers*, 2011
20 x 4 cm
Dagger glass beads, rondelles, seed beads;
right angle weave, herringbone stitch
Photo by Todd Keitel

B *Impending Bloom*, 2011
16 x 16 x 1 cm
Seed beads, fire-polished beads, crystals,
antique tricycle reflector, drilled copper washer,
precision mechanized gears, vintage sequins,
gunmetal ball chain; right angle weave, peyote
stitch, chevron netting, embroidery, drilling,
and dapping, wirework
Photo by Todd Keitel

B

ALL OF YOUR PIECES ARE RICHLY ELEGANT YET USE UNUSUAL ELEMENTS. DO YOU HAVE A STASH OF THE UNEXPECTED TO DRAW FROM?
I have an extensive stash supporting two distinct paths. One is a collection of beach findings, including boat parts, bones, and unidentified textured materials from my daily hikes along the Pacific Ocean. The second stash consists of mechanical parts my husband, a medical device engineer, has gifted to me. I also have a large collection of champagne foil-tops, small tins, and game pieces that I hope to incorporate into the next chapter of my work.

DO YOU HAVE A MUSE?
Observing nature, specifically color in nature, is the driving force of inspiration in my work. I have also found that having a defined theme or goal when I begin a necklace design leads to easier choices.

IN ADDITION TO JEWELRY, WHAT OTHER TYPES OF ARTWORK DO YOU ENJOY VIEWING?
I am inspired when I look at paintings and graphic design. I admire painters who can create an unconfined flow through effortless strokes.

A *The March Hare*, 2012
35.5 x 14 x 23 cm
Ceramic hare head, copper wire, seed beads, hand-dyed ribbon,
crystals, crystal chain, feathers, silk ribbon, vintage watch parts,
enameled parts; wire wrapping, right angle weave, peyote stitch
Photo by Todd Keitel

B

C

B *Royal Shore*, 2012
13 x 18 x 1 cm
Seed beads, bicones, pearls, rondelles,
crystal pendant, mother- of- pearl,
thread; right angle weave, chevron
netting, embroidery
Photo by Todd Keitel

C *Santa Catalina*, 2012
12 x 16 x 2.5 cm
Seed beads, glass cabochons, shells, beach glass,
crystals, rondelles, gemstones, pearls; right angle
weave, peyote stitch, bead embroidery
Photo by Todd Keitel

WHAT WORDS DESCRIBE YOUR CREATIVE METHOD?

The first ones that spring to mind are organized chaos. The second oxymoron would be rustic contemporary. There is a certain type of movement I try to create that is not kinetic, but more of a visual balance that moves your eye from one end of the piece to the other.

HOW DO YOUR DESIGNS PROCEED ONCE YOU HAVE YOUR IDEAS?

I most often begin with one object or strand of beads, then think about how I would like to support that object. Should it be the sole focus, or would it be better to look for interesting things that harmonize with it? I usually gather all the materials that could work color-wise with my idea, and then begin to work. I may have to backtrack and take things apart that don't work, but that is part of the process. If I take a quick photo, I can return to that idea later.

WHAT IS YOUR EXPERIENCE WITH THE INTERNET, AND HOW HAS IT INFLUENCED YOUR WORK?

The explosion of Pinterest has played the most exciting role in my bead art. Viewing such an abundance of gorgeous pieces inspires me and motivates me to try new techniques. I have also started a blog on the creative process, describing my agonies and delights.

HAS THE INTERNET HELPED YOU IN OTHER WAYS?

I feel connected to a circle of bead artists simply from reading blogs and viewing their work on-line. I know that a small comment or an acknowl-edgement about their work can be encouraging, so I try to do that. One well-known bead teacher once encouraged me after I had received a rejection letter by announcing on Facebook that she felt the piece was worthy. It meant a great deal to me.

IS JEWELRY YOUR EXCLU-SIVE FOCUS, OR DO YOU WORK IN ADDITIONAL FORMS OF BEADWORK?

The only finished pieces I currently have are jewelry, but I have begun some sculptural pieces that I intend to finish. This is definitely stimulating to think about, and maybe a little intimidating. It's exciting because the chal-lenge is to discover how to cover unusual surfaces with beads, so that will take some experimentation.

WHICH MATERIALS ARE YOU MOST ATTRACTED TO FOR YOUR BEADING?

I enjoy so many different elements that this will sound contradictory. For instance, I love glass and crystals and gemstones, yet matte finishes and rusty things always catch my eye. My passion is fueled by the allure of dis-covering new and unique beading materials.

A *Arrogant Bastard*, 2012
13 x 18 x 2 cm
Fire-polished seed beads, shaped bottle cap, bronze chain, jump rings, drop beads; right angle weave, peyote stitch
Photo by Todd Keitel

B *Passion of the Pen*, 2010
12 x 16 x 2.4 cm
Precision mechanized gears,
dagger glass beads, seed
beads, crystals, vintage
sequins, triangles; braiding
weave, wirework
Photo by Todd Keitel

C *Keys to the Hops*, 2011
21 x 7 x 2 cm
Vintage keys, formed beer
caps, copper wire, copper ball
chain, painted flowers; painting, wire wrapping, dapping,
soldering
Photo by Todd Keitel

D *Maria Elena*, 2011
12 x 12 x 1 cm
Seed beads, nautilus
cabochon, shells, crystals,
gemstones, pearls; right angle
weave, peyote stitch, bead
embroidery
Photo by Todd Keitel

**WHAT ARE YOU THINKING
AS YOU CONSIDER MATE-
RIALS FOR A PIECE?**
I always strive for the best
quality, because ultimately
my time is worth much
more than the extra cost
of materials. Color rules if
seed beads are involved,
but I might choose beads
based on the technique
involved. Or I may con-
sider their ethnicity if I'm
trying to find harmonious
authenticity in the piece.

**IN WHAT WAYS DO YOU
SEE YOURSELF GROWING
AS AN ARTIST?**
I'm excited about collage
and using vintage items
and hardware to create
more three-dimensional
sculptural pieces. I also see
my jewelry becoming less
flat and more dimensional.
I would also like to explore
enameling as well.

**WHAT EMOTIONS DO
YOU WANT TO GENERATE
IN FOLKS WHO SEE
YOUR PIECES?**
I would like them to feel a
sense of casual elegance
and notice well-finished
custom details, but not feel
the piece looks overdone.

"Susan uses a wide
array of intriguing
materials to create
bold, beautiful, and
stunning art-to-wear
pieces."

—MARCIA DECOSTER

I was born in Kharkov, Ukraine, and have lived in Israel since 1997. I found my fondness for beading in 2006, and began working as a crafter, and later as a teacher, in an arts and crafts shop in 2007. I have since won several awards, including a second place in the Seed Bead Jewelry category in the Bead Dreams 2012 competition, and runner-up in the 2012 Battle of the Beadsmith competition.

annbraginsky.com

ann braginsky

"My beads are my paints and bricks, the elements I use to create and convey my ideas."

A *Amazon Pendant*, 2011
12 x 6 cm
Seed beads, crystals,
labradorite; peyote stitch,
embroidery, right angle weave
Photo by Igor Kruter

B *Bracelet Poppies*, 2010
18 x 5 cm
Seed beads, agate, aventurine,
cornelian, pearls; peyote stitch,
embroidery, Ndebele stitch
Photo by Igor Kruter

C & D *Samurai*, 2012
46 x 50 cm
Seed beads, crystals, silk,
leather; peyote stitch,
St. Petersburg chain,
embroidery
Photos by Igor Kruter

D

THE FIRST NECKLACE OF YOURS THAT I NO-TICED WAS SO VISUALLY DIFFERENT THAN ANY-THING I'D SEEN. WHERE DO YOUR IDEAS COME FROM?
Through my art I try to show new visions and images of being a woman. Creative ideas come from what I see and feel in the world around me, as well as from literature, music, and works of art.

DO YOU HAVE A GOAL YOU WANT TO ACHIEVE WITH YOUR ART?
The mission of the artist is to talk to the audience without words. There shouldn't be anything unclear or untold between the person who sees my artwork and me. I feel like I should always move forward and try to make things that no-body has created yet.

WHAT REACTIONS TO YOUR WORK PLEASE YOU THE MOST?
First of all I would like to create a "wow!" ef-fect. And then I want my viewers to feel the emotion I was trying to express with my design, whether it's sadness, joy, the beauty of nature, a sense of soaring, and so on.

HOW LONG HAVE BEADS BEEN YOUR MEDIUM FOR CREATING ART?

Well, I took my first steps in beadwork in 2006. I was a "fresh-man"—back then I did not realize all the opportunities and challenges I would find in this craft field.

DO YOU HAVE A REGULAR METHOD TO DEVELOP YOUR JEWELRY PIECES?

At the beginning I imagine the character or idea, and then draw some sketches. The most successful sketches will later be drawn in meticulous detail. Then I think about the technical aspects of making the piece, and also about color and material coordination. At the end, I analyze all these steps and determine how I'm going to make it real.

DO YOU PREFER CERTAIN MATERIALS TO OTHERS?

I like seed beads because they involve detailed work that I create from scratch. But I also use crystal elements, as well as silver and natural gems.

HOW DO YOU EMPLOY THE INTERNET IN YOUR BEAD ART?

I use the Internet as a huge library where everything can be found quickly, and I've had the

A *Rose Ashes*, 2010
30 x 20 cm
Seed beads, crystals, silver, leather, onyx, amethyst; peyote stitch, embroidery
Photo by Igor Kruter

B & C *New Age Valkyrie*, 2012
17 x 36 cm
Seed beads, crystals, silver, leather; peyote stitch, embroidery
Photos by Igor Kruter

D *Summer Garden Hairpin*, 2012
12 x 5 cm
Seed beads, crystals; peyote stitch, embroidery
Photo by Igor Kruter

B

C

opportunity to connect with many interesting and outstanding professionals. It has led to more creative plans for my future projects. I have also been invited to participate in demanding contests where I made designs that may not have been created without those challenges.

WHICH TECHNIQUES DO YOU STILL WANT TO EXPLORE?
Well, recently I began designing a collection of soutache jewelry. This fine technique looks simply gorgeous!

"Exquisite detail is evident in each of Ann's breathtaking pieces."
—MARCIA DECOSTER

D

A

heather collin

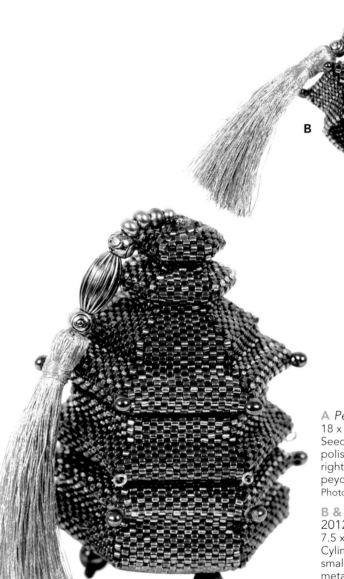

B

It was not long after I started bead stringing that I realized I wanted—no, needed—a far greater challenge. I put the Internet to good use, scouring sites for tutorials on how to advance. My first stitch was peyote. I did not realize I was working with size 15° seed beads, and I battled, unpicked, persisted, and finally got it right. I was so proud of that initial little sampler. And, I knew I had found what I was looking for. A passion was born!

beadingweavingpattern.com

C

A *Persian Tiles*, 2012
18 x 3 cm
Seed beads, glass pearls, fire-polished beads, nylon thread; right angle weave, tubular peyote stitch
Photo by Mike Helps

B & C *Wedding Ring Box*, 2012
7.5 x 4.5 cm
Cylinder beads, seed beads, small drops, glass pearls, metal beads, tassel, nylon thread; flat peyote and tubular peyote stitches
Photos by Mike Helps

"No notion or idea is set in stone—what I start with changes direction more often than not. It gets cut up, pulled apart, and restarted before I get to where I am happy with the flow of the design."

D *Vikings Prayer*, 2010
Necklace, 35 cm
Cylinder beads, seed beads, glass pearls, brass spacer and focal, thin cord, nylon thread; peyote stitch
Photo by Mike Helps

E *Faerie Lights*, 2012
48 cm
Seed beads, glass pearls, nylon thread; tubular herringbone stitch
Photo by Mike Helps

HOW LONG HAVE BEADS BEEN YOUR MEDIUM FOR CREATING ART?
I started with beads in March 2007.

I LOVE THE STRUCTURE AND TEXTURE IN YOUR WORK. DO YOU ATTRIBUTE THAT TO A PARTICULAR STITCH?
Yes I do, and that would be cubic right angle weave. If I work in other stitches, I tend to add layers to create texture.

CAN YOU PUT A LABEL OR CATEGORY ON YOUR TYPE OF WORK?
I would put most of my work under the "World Ethnic" banner, with a few deviations here and there.

WHERE DO YOU DERIVE YOUR CREATIVE INSPIRATION?
From anywhere, really. I write beading patterns and am more often than not inspired by the needs of my customers. I try to create items that are not too expensive to make and that are easy to wear— day-to-day jewelry.

DO OTHER MEDIA CONTRIBUTE TO YOUR ARTISTIC VISION?
Yes, I've used paint, cloth, wood, and currently ceramics. In each case the medium has dictated the outcome.

THE INTERNET HAS BEEN A BIG BENEFIT FOR MANY ARTISTS. HOW HAS IT PLAYED A ROLE IN YOUR BEAD ART?

The Internet is two-fold for me. The first is that I use it to market and sell my patterns as well as share pictures, primarily on Facebook, of my creations. The second is that I can keep up with what all the other beaders are doing. Being in different countries separates us; the Internet brings us together.

HAVE YOU DEVELOPED IMPORTANT ONLINE RELATIONSHIPS THAT ENHANCE YOUR BEADING?

The most critical relationship I have is with my pattern tester. She started as a customer and I later approached her to become my tester. There are, however,

A *Guinevere Necklace*, 2011
25 cm
Seed beads, glass pearls, filigree focal, fire-polished beads, nylon thread; cubic right angle weave
Photo by Mike Helps

B *Hindia*, 2012
22 cm
Seed beads, glass pearls, bicones, nylon thread; right angle weave
Photo by Mike Helps

C *Corset Cuff*, 2012
40.5 x 18 cm
Seed beads, fire-polished beads, nylon thread; right angle weave
Photo by Mike Helps

D *Butterfly Clasp*, 2010
Clasp section 8 x 3.5 cm
Cylinder beads, fire-polished beads, press studs, nylon thread; peyote stitch
Photo by Mike Helps

E *Evolutions*, 2011
23.6 x 2.5 cm each
Seed beads, nylon thread; tubular peyote stitch
Photo by Mike Helps

D

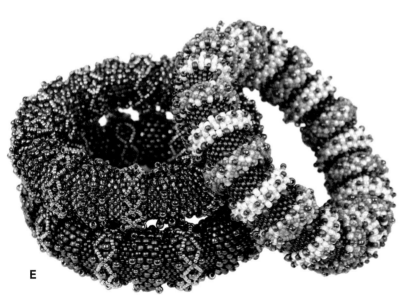

E

others that are also important to me. We are able to communicate online both publicly and privately, and they let me know when I am on the right design path.

ARE YOU INTERESTED IN A VARIETY OF ARTISTIC MEDIA?
Yes, polymer clay and bead embroidery fascinate me.

WHICH BEAD TECHNIQUES WOULD YOU LIKE TO WORK WITH MORE?
Bead embroidery, and possibly soutache.

IS YOUR MAIN FOCUS ON JEWELRY, OR ARE THERE ADDITIONAL FORMS OF BEADWORK IN YOUR BODY OF WORK?
I focus on jewelry, but I do get sidetracked now and then. For example, I love beading little shaped boxes!

WOULD YOU LIKE YOUR CUSTOMERS TO DERIVE ANY PARTICULAR SENSE FROM YOUR PIECES?
I would say touchabilty and happiness.

"Heather's distinctive style and craftsmanship are easily recognized in each of her wonderfully textured pieces."

—MARCIA DECOSTER

I am a beadwork artist and teacher based in Israel. I was born in Milan and grew up in London, where I graduated with a degree in fashion design. My interest in fashion has a great influence on my beadwork. My work has been showcased in a variety of publications over the years, and I've earned worldwide recognition through a distinct style that I describe as modern and chic. I enjoy exploring the fusion of materials and textures—for example, blending bead embroidery with leather and with metal work.

trizdesigns.com

A

patrizia tager

B

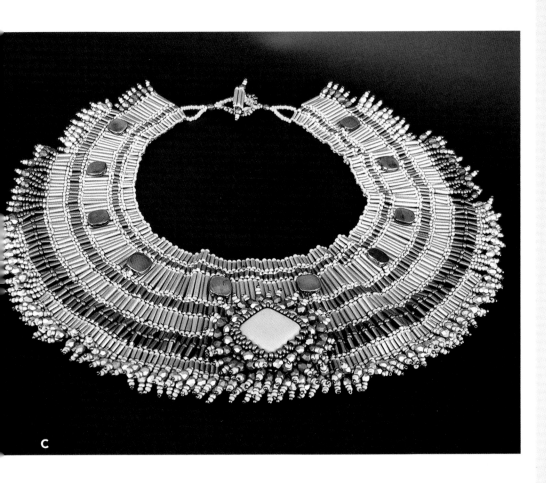

C

"There are three criteria I look for when choosing beads: quality, color, and texture. After that, it is all about how they work together within a design."

A *Arearea "Joyousness,"* 2010
Purse: 20.5 x 23.5 x 3.5 cm; Strap: 56 cm
Ceramic cabochons, crystals, freshwater pearls, seed beads, bugle beads, synthetic suede, polyethylene thread, metal bag frame, adhesive; bead embroidery, peyote stitch, spiral stitch
Photo by artist

B *Indian Summer Cuff,* 2012
19 x 9 cm
Glass cabochons, crystals, seed beads, leather, aluminum, polyethylene thread, adhesive; bead embroidery
Photo by artist

C *Let My People Go,* 2008
45 x 8cm
Bugle beads, seed beads, mother-of-pearl beads, fire-polished glass beads, turquoise, polyethylene thread, adhesive; ladder stitch, bead embroidery
Photo by artist

YOUR PIECES ARE FULL OF STRONG, CLEAN LINES JUXTAPOSED WITH ORGANIC ELEMENTS. HOW DO YOU GO ABOUT FINDING THE UNIQUE COMPONENTS THAT ARE SO BEAUTIFULLY COMPLEMENTED BY YOUR STITCHING?
My main resource for both components and beads is the Internet. I'm a bit of an insomniac and I like searching the Internet for unique and beautiful components during those hours when sleep eludes me. My favorite components are natural stones and handmade ceramics that I collect from various bead artists.

WILL YOU CHARACTERIZE YOUR STYLE FOR US?
I would describe it as elegant-modern with a twist. I've always admired that old Hollywood glamour, as well as the great jewelry designers: Lalique, Cartier, Van Cleef & Arpels, to name a few. But my personal style is more rock-chick meets girl-about-town. I try to create glamour with an edge in my pieces.

IS THE INTERNET A TOOL FOR YOUR BEAD ART?
It has played an integral role. As a mostly self-taught bead artist, I initially used the Internet to

acquire information on techniques and materials and to generally acquaint myself with the world of beadwork. As a single mother with a baby, I could study these new techniques without leaving my home. The Internet also gave me an international platform where I could sell my work and tutorials. If not for the Internet and the wonderful, creative, generous world of beadwork artists, I would not be where I am today.

WHICH BEADING MATERIALS ARE YOUR FAVORITES?

The materials I'm most drawn to are semiprecious stones, pearls, crystals, handmade ceramics, leather, and, of course, seed beads.

IS THERE AN IDENTIFIABLE METHOD TO YOUR DESIGN PROCESS?

Most designs start as an idea, a mood; I then choose beads and components that fit that mood. I lay them all out and form groups that complement each other. I then reduce my selections through a process of elimination. This sometimes leads me to develop more than one design idea, and I place those groups that are not being used into

A *Peacock Necklace*, 2012
Choker: 48.5;
Pendant: 17 x 7 cm
Crystals, seed beads, silver-plated clasp, leather, waxed cord, polyethylene thread, adhesive; bead embroidery, peyote stitch, bead crochet
Photo by artist

B *A Hazy Shade of Winter*, 2010
Bag: 21.5 x 13 cm;
Strap: 20.5 cm
Ceramic cabochon, glass cabochons, crystals, seed beads, leather, synthetic suede, waxed cord, polyethylene thread, metal bag frame, adhesive; bead embroidery, peyote stitch, bead crochet, square stitch
Photo by artist

C *Queen Boudicca Necklace*, 2010
Choker: 40 cm;
Pendant: 15 x 8.6 cm
Ceramic cabochons, plastic cabochon, seed beads, semiprecious stone, synthetic suede, polyethylene thread, adhesive; bead embroidery, peyote stitch, herringbone stitch, square stitch
Photo by artist

D *Untitled*, 2011
Polymer cabochon by Janice Varley Abarbanel, crystal pearls, seed beads, leather covered cuff, synthetic suede, brass, polyethylene thread, adhesive; bead embroidery, peyote stitch
Photo by artist

baskets to be used at a later time. My chosen focal components now dictate how the design develops. I equate this process as painting with beads.

AMONG OTHER ARTISTIC MEDIA, WHERE DO YOU FIND INSIGHT?

Fine art, photography, sculpture, textiles, origami, and haute couture fashion are some of the media that inspire me, but the list is endless. All beauty and balance evoke inspiration.

WHICH BEAD TECHNIQUES WOULD YOU LIKE TO EXPLORE IN FUTURE WORK?

Exploring new bead techniques is something I do constantly, but I prefer to focus on the whole design and use whichever technique is most suitable to achieve the look I want, rather than fixate on new techniques. I want to continue using different combinations of techniques and materials and not limit myself to any specific techniques.

"Unique and unexpected shapes bring a huge visual interest to each of Patrizia's stunning examples of bead-embroidered jewelry."

—MARCIA DECOSTER

Born and raised in the USSR, I've been crafting all my life, but it's beading that fills me with a sense of accomplishment and integrity, and has proven a most amenable vehicle for translating inner vision to outer reality. I'm a proud member of the Bead Society of Greater New York and a member of the Torpedo Factory Artists' Association, working in my studio in Alexandria, Virginia. Passion for three-dimensional shapes fuels my creative spirit, and my choice of beadwork as a primary art medium has followed that same fascination.

mylovelybeads.com

A

zoya gutina

"Beading has become my key to the secret garden, my way down the rabbit hole, my looking glass. The process of designing a new piece of jewelry has struck me as magical."

B

A *Star Burst*, 2011
44 cm
Round seed beads, bugle beads, teardrop
beads, accent beads, amethyst and faceted
round beads, crystal pearls, ammonite; right
angle weave, peyote stitch, St. Petersburg chain
stitch, netting, embroidery, beading around
cabochons
Photo by artist

B *Lady Winter*, 2009
43 cm
Hand-painted black onyx pendant featuring
Winter by Alfons Mucha, round, cylinder, and
charlotte seed beads, bugle beads, black onyx
round beads, crystal pearls; peyote stitch, coral
stitch, right angle weave, netting, free-form,
Russian leaves, embroidery
Photo by artist

**YOUR FREE-FORM NECK-
LACES ARE DONE SO
BEAUTIFULLY. WILL YOU
SHARE ANY SECRETS FOR
INCLUDING BALANCE
AND FORM WHEN WORK-
ING FREELY?**
Perhaps you will smile
to hear about my secret:
I've never tried to bal-
ance the composition.
On the contrary, I want
to achieve a completely
asymmetrical piece. I can
only say that each item
is first being created in
the soul. Technically, a
piece is multilayered,
where the first layer is
like a sketch giving defi-
nition, and the second,
overlapping the first,
adjusts the final shape
and composition.

**WHAT IS THE BEST
DESCRIPTION OF YOUR
WORK?**
Two words: beaded jew-
elry. My bead artwork
is romantic in style, and
often three-dimensional
free-form in shape. It
leans toward the build-
ing of shapes and forms
that are functional and
wearable. My main
theme is nature, and I'm
getting closer and closer
to the aesthetics of
Art Nouveau.

**HOW LONG HAVE YOU
BEEN CREATING ART
WITH BEADS?**
I am very careful in the
choice of words like "art"
when I describe what I
make. I've been crafting
since my childhood, and
I learned beading when

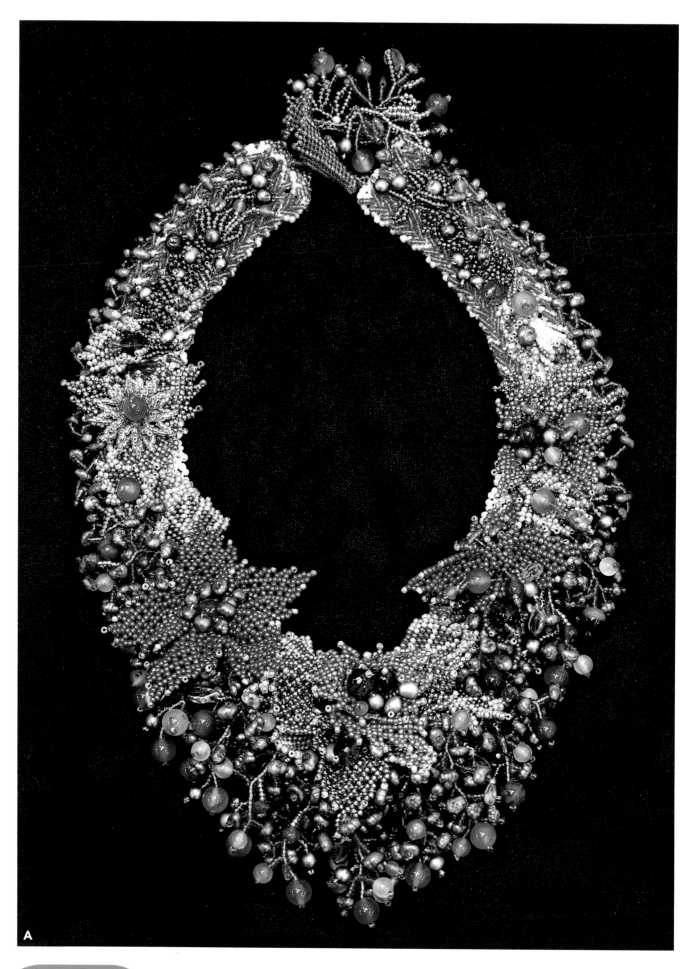

144

B

A *Lush Spring Blues*, 2009
43 cm
Round seed beads, pearls,
carnelian and fluorite round
beads, amethyst and faceted
round beads; peyote stitch,
coral stitch, netting, right
angle weave, embroidery
Photo by artist

B *Crystal Flowers*, 2010
43 cm
Round and cylinder seed
beads, bugle beads, teardrop
beads, clear quartz chips,
freshwater pearls, accent
beads, glass faceted beads,
glass faceted button; peyote
stitch, coral stitch, netting,
right angle weave, free-form,
Russian leaves, embroidery
Photo by artist

C *Christmas Eve*, 2009
45 cm
Round and cylinder seed
beads, vintage Italian bugle
beads, crystals, pearls, ribbons; peyote stitch, netting,
coral stitch, right angle weave,
embroidery
Photo by artist

C

I decorated my ballet dress
with beads. I started making
jewelry in 2002. Beadwork
is traditionally considered
as craft, but there is also a
term "fine craft" that actually means "art." The magical
process of beading led me
from hobby to art.

**HOW DIFFICULT IS IT TO
THINK OF IDEAS FOR YOUR
JEWELRY?**
Oh, inspiration comes from the
world around me and practi-
cally overwhelms me. I work
at an art center next to amazing artists whose works shout,
"Implement me in beads!" I
love all of nature: blossom-
ing flowers in spring, frozen
geometric shapes in winter, or
beautiful colors during sunrise
and sunset. Changing nature
stirs my emotions and captures
my spirit.

**HOW DO YOU DEVELOP
YOUR DESIGNS?**
Sometimes I sketch outlines,
but more often I just keep the
image of a piece of jewelry in
my mind. I think about style,
shape, color, materials, size, and
techniques before I start. Then I
weave the base, followed by the
other parts, making enough so
that later I have a choice. I fold
ready elements together and
rearrange them to achieve a
harmonious combination before
the final touches.

**IN TERMS OF BEADING, WHAT
ARE YOU EXCITED TO TRY
THAT YOU HAVEN'T DONE YET?**
I am trying to invent beading techniques to use in my
work. I hope to publish a
book and share my creative
secrets and inventions.

WHAT OTHER ARTS-AND-CRAFTS-TYPE ACCOMPLISHMENTS ARE IN YOUR BACKGROUND?

I'm an explorer and have learned that any experience is useful. I've been sewing, knitting, and crocheting for many years, and I've worked with felt, paper, and polymer clay. Crafting with yarn and fabric led me to weaving and working with patterns. When I used felt and clay, I learned principles of three-dimensional designs.

WHAT ARE YOUR FAVORITE MATERIALS TO WORK WITH?

Among my favorites are small round seed beads (especially the Czech charlotte beads). I like Japanese cylinder beads as well as all crystals, pearls, and glass beads. I like to experiment with various materials in my work, from ribbons and fabric to wood and metal.

WHAT TYPES OF BEADS DO YOU TYPICALLY USE?

The choice of beads for a particular piece of jewelry depends on my ideas about theme, style, and image. I strive to design items rich in texture, so I like combining matte and glossy beads of different shapes and sizes in one piece.

ARE YOU USING THE INTERNET TO ENHANCE YOUR BEADING ACTIVITY?

I've made literally thousands of online friends from all continents (except Antarctica—I'm kidding!). Thanks to the Internet, I can host the Fashion Colorworks

A *Under the Linden Trees*, 2010
43 cm
Maplewood cabochons, wooden beads, round seed beads, vintage Italian bugle beads, pearls; peyote stitch, coral stitch, netting, embroidery, beading around cabochons
Photo by artist

B *Poppy Field*, 2008
43 cm
Round seed beads, accent beads, teardrop beads, plastic flower clasp; right angle weave, peyote stitch, coral stitch, embroidery
Photo by artist

C

D

C *Art Nouveau Restored*, 2010
43 cm
Antique charlotte beads, round and cylinder seed beads, fire-polished beads, crystals, pearls; peyote stitch, coral stitch, square stitch, ladder stitch, right angle weave, Russian leaves, netting, embroidery
Photo by artist

D *Autumn Splendor*, 2008
42 cm
Cherry burl wood cabochons, wooden beads, round seed beads, bugle beads, pearls; peyote stitch, netting, embroidery, beading around cabochons
Photo by artist

Online Beading Contest that attracts hundreds of artists from all over the world, and I can send my English and Russian newsletters to thousands of subscribers.

HAS THE INTERNET HELPED THE BUSINESS ASPECT OF YOUR BEADING?
Several years ago the editors of the German magazine *Perlen Poesie* noticed my Facebook page. They suggested I prepare a tutorial for one of my projects, which they published. Now I've been invited several times to the Beaders Best Bead Show in Hamburg, Germany, to teach workshops.

WHAT KIND OF FEED-BACK DO YOU GET FROM VIEWERS?
I hear words of admiration, joy, and gratitude, and see the glowing eyes of my studio visitors. Their good feelings are my best rewards. They give me strength to work, and I want to offer my thanks to my viewers and customers.

"Queen of the collar, Zoya explores this classic form, bringing texture and movement to each of her pieces."

—MARCIA DECOSTER

A

I studied architecture before devoting myself to jewelry design, which is now my profession. I've completed courses in goldsmith, jewelry design, and fashion accessories from Altos de Chavon in the Dominican Republic, my home country, and FTI in New York. My creations have appeared in major Dominican publications, and I've made jewelry and accessories for fashion designers internationally. I am active in the Dominican fashion community and serve as an educator, giving workshops in jewelry design and fashion accessories. My creations combine common materials with unconventional ones.

edgarlopezdesign.com

edgar lópez

B

A *Link Earrings*, 2011
12 x 4 x 0.2 cm
Seed beads, cylinder beads, sterling silver links, crystals; brick stitch
Photo by Edgar Núñez

B *Bracelet from Caribbean Dream Collection*, 2012
17 x 5 x 1 cm
Seed beads, larimar and agate cabochons, crystals; cubic right angle weave, peyote stitch
Photo by Edgar Núñez

C *Caribbean Dream Necklace*, 2012
48 cm;
Bib: 11.4 x 22.2 cm
Seed beads, larimar cabochon, crystals, turquoise; cubic right angle weave, peyote stitch, brick stitch
Photo by Giovanni Cavallaro

C

"Not only is it important for people to see a beautiful piece of art, but I also want them to feel the emotion I put into every part of this creative process."

YOUR WORK SEEMS WONDERFULLY INFLUENCED BY YOUR FINE ARTS DEGREE. PLEASE TELL US ABOUT THAT CONNECTION.
I am an architect and a designer of fashion jewelry. Definitely this combination has helped me establish an interesting vision to create designs and at the same time develop visual harmony.

GIVE US A BRIEF SUMMARY OF YOUR STYLE.
My work is eclectic—a mixture of color, shapes, and textures. I especially like to put a lot of detail in my pieces. Definitely, I'm nothing minimalist.

WHEN DID YOU START WORKING WITH BEADS?
I have ten years as a fashion jewelry designer, but only three using beads as a means of creating my art.

HOW HAS YOUR EXPERIENCE IN LIFE AFFECTED YOUR ART?
I'm from a tropical country. My work is heavily influenced by the details of nature and the color that surrounds me.

HOW DOES YOUR CREATIVE PROCESS TYPICALLY UNFOLD?
First, inspiration comes to me as an idea. Then, in the process of converting the idea into something tangible, I continue making subtle changes, looking for the best way to build what I envisioned. I am always trying to

A

A *Link Necklace*, 2011
16 x 4 x 0.5 cm
Seed beads, cylinder beads,
crystals, sterling silver links;
brick stitch
Photo by Edgar Núñez

B *Tropical Earrings*, 2012
9.5 x 4 x 1.2 cm
Seed beads, crystals, cabochons; cubic right angle
weave, peyote stitch
Photo by Edgar Núñez

C *Mystic Earrings*, 2011
10.5 x 4 x 0.5
Tila beads, seed beads, crystals, gold chain; tila work
Photo by Edgar Núñez

D *The Chameleon
Necklace*, 2012
18 x 4 x 1.5 cm
Seed beads, turquoise, crys-
tals; cubic right angle weave
Photo by Edgar Núñez

E *Maya Earrings*, 2011
10 x 4 x 0.5 cm
Seed beads, cabochons,
crystals, tila beads, turquoise,
cylinder beads; peyote stitch,
tila work
Photo by Edgar Núñez

F *The Doll Earrings*, 2012
4 x 4 x 1 cm
Seed beads, crystals;
netting stitch
Photo by Edgar Núñez

B

C

D

E

F

achieve a piece that is not only beautiful, but also comfortable and harmonious.

AS A BEAD ARTIST, HOW HAS THE INTERNET EN-HANCED YOUR WORK?

The Internet has definitely made a difference as a means to share my work with the world. Because I live in a Caribbean country, the Internet is a very important tool for me. It would have been very difficult for me to take my work around the world, but thanks to the Internet, it is possible for people as far away as France, Japan, India, or Italy to know my work.

WHAT ABOUT PEOPLE YOU'VE MET ONLINE?

I have made good friends and have shared ideas. I recently participated in an online contest where I met many designers from around the world. To see their work and compare ideas with them has helped me grow as a professional.

DO OTHER FORMS OF ARTISTIC MEDIA IN-SPIRE YOUR JEWELRY?

Music definitely helps inspire me, but above all, artwork, photography, and fashion. I'm a very visual person.

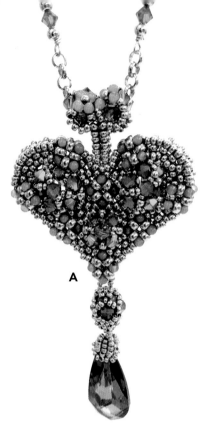

A *The Royal Heart,* 2012
8 x 5 x 1 cm
Seed beads, crystals, round
blue jade; cubic right
angle weave
Photo by Edgar Núñez

B *Nefertiti Necklace,* 2011
16 x 8 x 1 cm
Turquoise, coral, seed beads,
crystals, gold chain; right
angle weave
Photo by Edgar Núñez

C *Romantic Land
Necklace,* 2012
16 x 7 x 1 cm
Seed beads, jade, crystals,
ribbon; right angle weave
Photo by Edgar Núñez

WHICH BEAD TECHNIQUES DO YOU MOST ENJOY?

Currently, I'm in love with right angle weave and cubic right angle weave, because they give me the freedom to build in a lot of different ways. In the future, I would like to mix beadweaving with other techniques of jewelry.

HOW DO YOU STRIVE TO MAKE AN EMOTIONAL IMPACT ON YOUR VIEWERS?

I design with love and passion, and I hope those qualities are reflected in the final result. I want people who see my work to feel this.

WHICH MATERIALS ARE WE GOING TO SEE MOST OFTEN IN YOUR JEWELRY?

I love using crystals, pearls, and different types of gemstones. Currently, I have been using a lot of amber and larimar gemstones that come from my country, although I always try to use them in an innovative manner, coming from a different point of view.

WHAT LEADS YOU TO CHOOSE CERTAIN BEADS?

I choose beads depending on the type of design idea I have in my mind, but I always focus on the quality that the piece will have when it is completed.

"Edgar's fine arts degree is apparent as you experience his elegantly styled earrings, necklaces, and bracelets, many of which are red-carpet worthy."

—MARCIA DECOSTER

D *Geometric Pendant,* 2012
12 x 3.5 x 1 cm
Seed beads,
cabochons, crystal, gold chain;
cubic right angle weave
Photo by Edgar Núñez

E *The Colorful
Earrings,* 2012
8 x 3 x 1 cm
Seed beads, cylinder beads,
turquoise,
sterling silver; cubic right
angle weave
Photo by Edgar Núñez

F *The Garden
Earrings,* 2012
8.5 x 4 x 1.5 cm
Seed beads, cabochon,
crystals; cubic right angle weave,
peyote stitch
Photo by Edgar Núñez

G *Bohemian
Pendant,* 2011
13 x 6.5 x 1.2 cm
Seed beads, cabochons, gold chain,
turquoise, crystals; right angle weave
Photo by Edgar Núñez

about marcia decoster

I live in a wonderful Art Deco home in San Diego with my husband, Mark, whose enduring encouragement has allowed me to pursue my career as a bead artist. For someone who loves beading, jewelry, travel, and people, I've found the ideal line of work!

My love for beautiful jewelry, along with a life-long passion to create my own designs, led me to discover beads in the 1990s. After spending those early years learning and developing fundamental skills, I soon found myself gravitating to right angle weave in much of my work, becoming a full-time bead artist by 2004. I love to design colorful and fun-to-wear jewelry.

These days, in addition to design work, I spend my time writing, teaching, and sharing the joy of beads with friends around the world. My work has been published in Carol Wilcox Wells's book, *The Art & Elegance of Beadweaving*, and was showcased in *Masters: Bead-weaving*. In addition, I have authored *Marcia DeCoster's Beaded Opulence*, a volume in Lark's Beadweaving Master Class series, as well as the recent *Beads in Motion*.

I was honored in 2009 to be chosen by *Beadwork* magazine as a Designer of the Year, and am proud to be recognized as a top ten teacher at the 2010 Bead & Button Show.

marciadecoster.com

maddesignsbeads.blogspot.com

A

B

C

A *Dream Keeper Vessel Rings*, 2013
2.5 x 5 x 1.2 cm
Seed beads, crystals, navette fancy stones;
right angle weave, embellishment
Photo by Marcia DeCoster

B *Spirit Flight*, 2012
7.6 x 5 cm
Seed beads, crystals, rivoli, wooden ball, silk ribbon;
Ndebele stitch, ladder stitch,
Photo by Marcia DeCoster

C *Pacific Morning Glory Earrings, 2013*
3.8 x 1.3 cm
Seed beads, crystals, pearls, ear wires; Ndebele
stitch, ladder stitch
Photo by Marcia DeCoster

D *Ringlets*, 2009
3.2 cm each
Seed beads, crystals, aluminum rings, glass rings;
right angle weave
Photo by Marcia DeCoster

E *Pacific Morning Glory Pendant*, 2013
6.3 x 6.3 x 1.3 cm
Seed beads, crystals, pave crystallized bead;
Ndebele stitch, ladder stitch
Photo by Marcia DeCoster

F *Pacific Morning Glory Pendant,
reverse side, 2013*
6.3 x 6.3 x 1.3 cm
Seed beads, crystals, pave crystallized bead;
Ndebele stitch, ladder stitch
Photo by Marcia DeCoster

D

E

F

A

B

A *Vienna,* 2012
12.7 x 8.9 cm
Seed beads, crystals, pearls,
chain, pave crystal drops,
silk ribbon; cubic right angle
weave
Photo by Marcia DeCoster

B *Playing with Possibilities
Components,* 2013
assorted sizes
Seed beads, crystals, pearls;
Ndebele stitch, cubic right
angle weave, ladder stitch
Photo by Marcia DeCoster

C *Pacific Morning Glory
Bracelet,* 2012
17.8 x 5.1cm
Seed beads, crystals, pearls;
Ndebele stitch, right angle
weave
Photo by Marcia DeCoster

C

D *Locket, 2013*
5 x 2.5 x 1.3 cm
Seed beads, crystals, key;
cubic right angle weave,
peyote stitch, right
angle weave
Photo by Marcia DeCoster

E *Locket, heart side, 2013*
5 x 2.5 x 1.3 cm
Seed beads, crystals, key;
cubic right angle weave,
peyote stitch, right
angle weave
Photo by Marcia DeCoster

F *Pacific Morning Glory Ring,
2013*
8.9 x 3.8 cm
Seed beads, crystals, pave
crystallized bead; Ndebele stitch,
ladder stitch
Photo by Marcia DeCoster

D

E

F

additional photo credits

Thank you to the following photographers who took portraits of the artists featured in this book:

Pinda Bazley, page 6

Neva Brown, page 16

Carrie Austin Photography, page 20

Shawn Haley, page 30

Terry Stephan, page 36

Tony Nolan, page 42

John Michael, page 48

Sherwood Lake Photography, page 52

Christian Daitche/FOTOBONN, page 58

Eric Lim, page 62

Martin Chivers, page 66

Frank Schmole, page 70

Paul Machael Olckers, page 76

Avi Lam, page 86

Christian Daitche, page 92

Kate McKinnon, page 102

Jeroen Medema, page 110

Harry Gilbert, page 116

Monique Georgette Lucienne Dilly Hale, page 120

Todd Keitel, page 124

Viktor Petrenko, page 130

Mike Helps, page 134

Dawn Aitman, page 138

Edgar Núñez, page 148

The following artists took self portraits:

Miriam Shimon, page 10

Melissa Ingram, page 24

Cynthia Newcomer Daniel, page 80

Marsha Wiest-Hines, page 96

Linda L. Jones, page 106

Zoya Gutina, page 142

acknowledgments

Thanks go to Nathalie Mornu who first conceived of *Marcia DeCoster Presents* as a way of showcasing the artistry of beadweaving. Kevin Kopp was instrumental in providing the organization required when working with the large number of images and artists in this collection.

Huge thanks go to the many artists who trusted me to present their images in this volume of contemporary beadweaving. Over the course of the last few years, I have developed many relationships whose common thread has been the love of beads. A large beading community resides online, and a number of these relationships started there by making a Facebook friend or reading a fascinating blog. I've since had wonderful opportunities to meet many of these folks in my travels and am in awe of their collective talent.

I am honored that each of the artists presented here are willing to share their talents to be enjoyed by many. Many thanks to each of you!

Marcia DeCoster
Something Fishy, 2013
19 x 7.6 x 2.5 cm
Fish leather, filigree, seed beads, crystal, loch rose, corrugated brass; Ndebele stitch, ladder stitch
Photo by artist

index

Marcia DeCoster
Bollywood Cuff, 2013
19 x 7.6 x 1.3 cm
Seed beads, crystals, navette fancy stone;
right angle weave, embellishment
Photo by artist

More Beading Books for the Artist in You

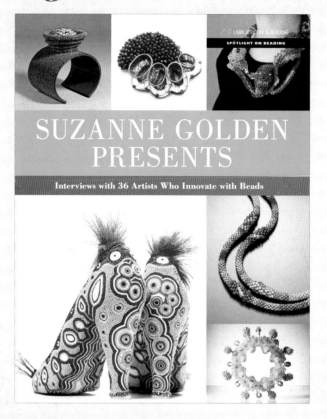

This best-selling volume kicks-off Lark's Spotlight on Beading series. It includes interviews with 36 innovative artists who show you their most beautiful and compelling work. Curated by Suzanne Golden, this will provide inspiration to explore new designs.

Also from Marcia DeCoster

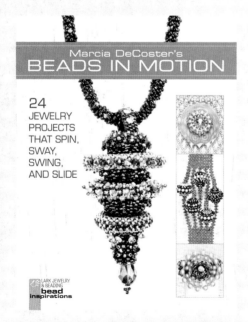

Marcia brings a sense of playfulness, sophistication, and dynamism to jewelry by exploring the art of motion. Many of the 24 projects found here swing, slide, or spin. She uses a variety of stitches, with diagrams and step-by-step instructions to illustrate each.

Marcia presents more than 20 magnificent contemporary jewelry projects to make with right angle weave. Beautifully photographed, this book is complete with a wonderful gallery of work from other important artists.